WAGGY TAILS & WHEELCHAIRS

The complete guide
to harmonious
living for you and
your dog

Alexander Epp

Hubble & Hattie

For more than eighteen years, the folk at Veloce have concentrated their publishing efforts on all-things automotive. Now, in a break with tradition, the company launches a new imprint for a new publishing genre!

The Hubble & Hattie imprint – so-called in memory of two, much-loved West Highland Terriers – will be the home of a range of books that cover all things animal, all produced to the same high quality of content and presentation as our motoring books, and offering the same great value for money.

More titles from Hubble & Hattie

Complete Dog Massage Manual, The – Gentle Dog Care (Robertson)
Dinner with Rover (Paton-Ayre)
Dog Games – stimulating play to entertain your dog and you (Blenski)
Dog Relax – relaxed dogs, relaxed owners (Pilguj)
Know Your Dog – The guide to a beautiful relationship (Birmelin)
My dog is blind – but lives life to the full! (Horsky)
Smellorama – nose games for dogs (Theby)
Waggy Tails & Wheelchairs (Epp)
Winston ... the dog who changed my life (Klute)
You and Your Border Terrier – The Essential Guide (Alderton)
You and Your Cockapoo – The Essential Guide (Alderton)

Currency calculator
At the time of publication, a unit of currency ● equals approximately
£1.00/US$1.50/euro 1.10

Translated by Anna McLuckie

WWW.HUBBLEANDHATTIE.COM

First published in May 2010 by Veloce Publishing Limited, Veloce House, Parkway Farm Business Park, Middle Farm Way, Poundbury, Dorchester, Dorset, DT1 3AR, England.
Fax 01305 250479/e-mail info@veloce.co.uk/web www.veloce.co.uk or www.velocebooks.com.
Original publication © 2009 Kynos Verlag, Dr Dieter Fleig GmbH. www.kynos-verlag.de
ISBN: 978-1-845842-92-5 UPC: 6-36847-04292-9
Readers with ideas for books about animals, or animal-related topics, are invited to write to the editorial director of Veloce Publishing at the above address.
British Library Cataloguing in Publication Data – A catalogue record for this book is available from the British Library. Typesetting, design and page make-up all by Veloce Publishing Ltd on Apple Mac. Printed in India by Imprint Digital.

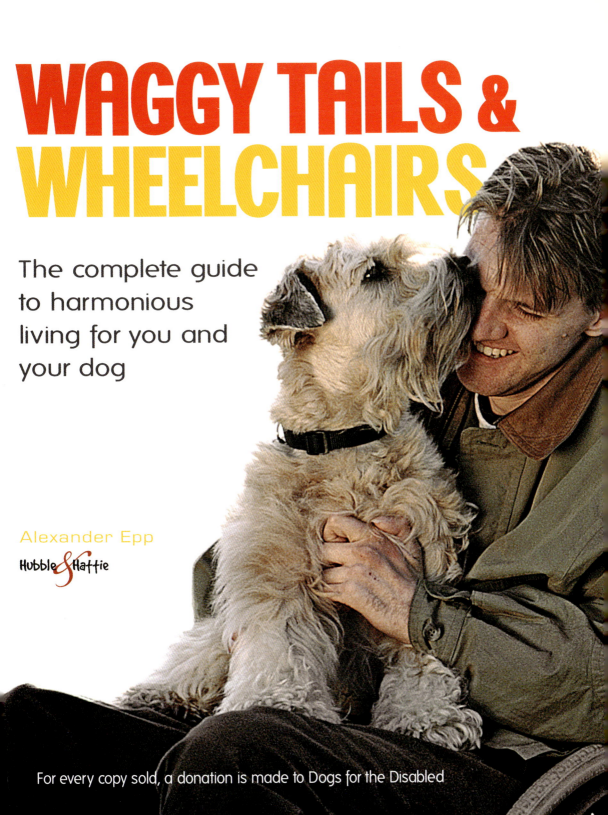

WAGGY TAILS & WHEELCHAIRS

The complete guide to harmonious living for you and your dog

Alexander Epp

Hubble & Hattie

For every copy sold, a donation is made to Dogs for the Disabled

About the book

Dog ownership for the mobility impaired is governed by more or less the same rules as those for the able-bodied, and neither group of individuals needs to do an adult education course to enable them to successfully co-exist with their four-legged friend. However, as the situation of the mobility impaired dog owner may give cause for concern in respect of certain aspects, it is important to address some issues long before actually acquiring a dog.

In this book, I discuss the most significant of the differences to conventional dog ownership arrangements, and also concentrate on companion dogs rather than service dogs. I have not included areas such as dogs and illness, or canine nutrition, which are the same regardless of the owner's degree of mobility. In the chapter headed Training, I do deal with areas where it is preferable to deviate from standard training methods and goals.

The object of this book is to provide you with guidance in making your decision, not a recommendation to share your life, whatever the cost, with an extremely agile and mobile canine. My aim is allow you, dear reader, to formulate a realistic idea about whether you are able and willing, in your specific situation, to take on dog ownership, given the considerations and issues that this entails.

About the author

Alexander Epp was born in 1967, and has been reliant on a wheelchair since the age of 21.

He couldn't – and didn't want to – imagine life without a dog, and was accompanied on numerous extensive tours by village dogs and strays, who joined him voluntarily.

Alexander's previous book, *Friendship instead of dominance – forging a relationship with your dog without shackles*, caused a sensation among the experts …

Beloved Ferro: 30 March 2001-17 December 2007

Contents

Fundamental considerations

BASIC REQUIREMENTS

We'll tackle the most important question straight away: do you live with somebody who could take a dog for walks? Because if you do, virtually none of the issues discussed in the following pages need apply.

If you live alone, but have your own garden then you are also going to be spared the most difficult obstacles with which dog ownership may present you. However, even if one of these scenarios matches yours, you may still want to take care of your dog yourself, which will include ensuring that he or she gets adequate exercise. On the other hand, if you live by yourself in a rented flat with no garden, not very nice neighbours, a crazy landlord, and an obstreporous caretaker, then you probably really need the friendship that a dog can provide – but this means you will also have the biggest problems to deal with.

You have to be able to meet a dog's regular requirements all year round: no one should ever entertain ideas such as "Let's see how we go. If it doesn't work out, we'll just give the dog away." Spend time looking into the issues set out here before making your decision; you may then come to realise that it's just not possible (yet) for you to have your own dog in your current situation. Love may indeed know no boundaries, but, under some circumstances, a considered decision *not* to get your own dog is a better expression of love for animals than forcing together two factors which will only fit well under very specific conditions: these factors being a wheelchair/mobility scooter user and owning a dog.

First of all, consider what sort of dog you would like. A little helper, who does your laundry, cooks pizza, and chews up your mobile? Or maybe you're looking for a friend to cuddle up with on rainy afternoons and take out on sunny days? Don't forget: a dog doesn't rehabilitate you, he puts extra strain on you!

Before you consider getting a dog, you need to have completed your basic rehabilitation, both physically and in terms of becoming used to getting around in a wheelchair or mobility scooter. You also need to have a suitable wheelchair/scooter and appropriate, functional clothing. Subsequently, a four-legged friend will be able to help you refine certain areas of your physical rehabilitation and improve your state of health. It makes particular sense for someone who is mobility-impaired to live with a dog, as they are even more likely than able-bodied people to think it's too cold/ wet/ windy to go out today. An extended period of physical activity in the fresh air is without doubt extremely beneficial to the individual who otherwise spends the entire day sitting or lying down, and whose circulation will be incredibly sluggish as a result. Moreover, dealing with the different needs of a canine can have a positive influence on the approach to one's own physical 'difference.' It's my opinion, however, that a dog will be a loyal companion for a nature lover, but will soon become too much of a burden for a city dweller.

YOUR PHYSICAL CONSTITUTION

Ask yourself (and answer really honestly): what is the current state of my physical health? A dog has to be looked after every day, and this means no days off, or weekends off, or holidays. Do you think you are up to that? Do you know anyone who would be able to take your dog out for you on days when health problems prevent you from doing so?

The more dependent you are, the greater the precariousness of the situation. A walker-rollator user has the fallback option of using

a wheelchair, should his wheeled rollator develop a fault, or his health take a turn for the worse, which at least ensures that he can still take his dog out. A wheelchair user could only opt to use an electric wheelchair in similar circumstances, assuming that he has one at his disposal. It is unlikely that someone who can only get around using an electric wheelchair would have a second one available for emergencies, and it is at this point that a knock-on effect will mean your obligations cannot be met.

How stable is your health situation? Are you laid low in bed with the flu at the first sign of snow? Will you be strong enough to cope with going out every day in winter? Remember that you could be outside in extremely cold conditions for some time, which you may not have done before. Poor health can improve, of course, but yours needs to have stabilised before you get a dog. The chronically ill wheelchair/scooter user must take into account that he will not be able to take his dog out on some wet days or when there is heavy snow. Even an able-bodied dog owner becomes ill from time-to-time, but this eventuality doesn't have to be factored in every year without fail. On no account should you just decide: "Oh yes, I can do that, no problem."

My advice would be that you put yourself through a test phase lasting at least a month, spending one or two hours outside every day. Anyone who hasn't always had a routine of going out every day may experience physical difficulties undertaking a sudden change to three walks a day.

Do you have the kind of chronic illness problems that mean you have to spend several weeks in hospital, and/or a rehabilitation centre every six months? These are not ideal conditions for dog ownership.

You also need to consider the following in view of all the times that you will be walking your dog – preferably in the countryside. Are you able to get yourself back into your wheelchair/scooter without any help after you have fallen out of it? On rough terrain this happens to me almost every month. You are going to be out and about during the evening, in the dark and in freezing temperatures, so may not come across anyone who would be able to help you. Have you ever patched up a flat tyre in dark, freezing, wet conditions? (Not something that anyone with a limited grip function could do.) You could rely on your mobile to summon help, but how will you survive the wait until help arrives without succumbing to hypothermia? If necessary, when you encounter problems that you cannot resolve by yourself, you need to be able to draw on auxiliary resources or helpers.

Do you tend to sleep late in the mornings? Remember that, being mobility-impaired, you will need to allow more time to get yourself ready to go out in the morning. Are you already pushed to the full extent of your physical resources? Someone who is not operating at the full extent of his or her physical capabilities will perhaps have no trouble at all in dealing with the extra effort that a dog entails, but there just may not be that extra capability to draw on.

Typically, a dog needs complete commitment from his owner, and you may have little energy left to spare as a result; no buffer zone on which to draw for any unexpected additional exertion or illness. It's important to take this into consideration.

TIME ISSUES

Reckon on devoting 10 per cent of your time each day to your dog (which may turn out to be 100 per cent of your leisure time!) Allow for two one-hourly walks every day, and factor in half an hour for preparation beforehand and sorting out time afterwards: for instance, on a rainy day, you will need to change out of your wet clothes and hang them up somewhere to dry, spend time wiping up the water that will have already accumulated in the hallway, dry your dog, and carry out numerous other associated tasks. The able-bodied will achieve these things in next to no time, but they take even the most active wheelchair user far longer, and a rainy day will double the time involved. In the winter, looking after the dog and the house can become a full-time job for a self-reliant individual.

The course of your day will be punctuated by the need to walk your dog, which can also mean that your life runs according to a very strict rhythm. A wide variety of opinion exists on the subject of how long the walks should be: some experts say that 3 miles a day is more than sufficient for a German Shepherd, but, in my experience, a medium-sized dog needs quite a bit more than this to get enough exercise and be happy. The regime recommended by extremists, who claim that you must do five walks of at least an hour each, means that you are just training your dog to be dissatisfied and putting immense pressure on yourself, thereby doing neither your dog nor you any good. So, you need to find a middle path that will suit your individual circumstances.

Will you be able to manage to fit all of this into your current schedule? Are you ready to invest all this time in a dog, even if it means making concessions elsewhere? It is, of course, very nice to always have someone with you in what used to be an empty house, and to be greeted joyously every morning. But if your dog makes you feel constantly stressed and overloaded, he is not going to enrich your life, no matter how much of an animal lover you are.

I would like to add a couple of points of reference from my own experience.

All the medium-sized dogs that I have had were happy to sleep 14 hours a night. In the morning, they always had a good sniff around before finding a place to relieve themselves. It is plainly quite possible to integrate all human requirements for sleep with keeping a dog.

During the day, an eight-hour period between walks is not a problem. It is also true to say that the three walks a day that are generally regarded as compulsory are, in fact, by no means necessary; my four-hour afternoon excursions are an amalgamation of morning and afternoon walks. Dog ownership need not entail taking your four-legged friend out first thing at six in the morning and sauntering around the village for the last time after ten o'clock every evening.

WORK

Clearly, if you work, this is an area with time considerations. On the one hand, working provides you with the financial wherewithal for keeping a dog, but, on the other, it may limit your time so much that it makes dog ownership an impossibility.

Anyone who is out of the house all day and can't take his dog with him should forget about having a dog of their own. If you are currently living an enforced life of 'leisure,' supporting yourself on benefits, a pension, savings or insurance payments, this could change and force you to consider rehoming your canine friend. If you work from home or are a freelancer, keeping a dog poses few problems, as it won't be necessary to leave him for hours on end. And if he needs to relieve himself, you are available to take him out. Some employers allow you to take your dog to work.

I would suggest a ballpark figure of ●50 a month for the upkeep of a medium-sized dog, although even a mild illness or injury could eat up your entire annual budget. Therefore, put as much effort as possible into stabilising your work and financial position as much as your health situation before considering getting a dog.

YOUR LIVING ARRANGEMENTS

What are your living circumstances like? Do you have neighbours who will take you to court the first time they hear barking? In any multi-occupancy building, a decision prohibiting keeping animals may be taken at any time, should the majority vote in favour of this. And in these circumstances, regardless of whether you are an owner-occupier or a tenant, you will have to either rehome your dog or move out. A disabled owner can cite specific hardships in his defence, and an exceptional need for keeping a dog. If there are already several dog owners amongst your neighbours, you are on somewhat safer ground; after all, none of these owners is going to vote for a ban, which makes it less likely that there will be a majority vote in favour of this.

If you are a tenant, you will have to ask even more people for their permission. It is always advisable to closely examine the small print in your tenancy agreement and house rules as regards the keeping of animals, and discuss the subject with your landlord and caretaking staff in advance.

Is your apartment spacious enough for a dog *and* a wheelchair/scooter? An apartment with 30 square metres of floor space has so little room to move that getting a dog is really out of the question. And a dachshund really will require just as much of the living space as a German Shepherd!

Where do you currently live? Is there somewhere that you can get to fairly easily and quickly so that your dog can relieve himself, or would this mean packing dog and wheelchair/scooter into the car? Is there a field that you and your dog can get to in a few minutes so that he can have a bit of a run around? Consider whether you really want to get a dog if you live in the centre of a large city, where suitable places for this are few and far between. Living on the edge of town or in the country makes this all so much easier. Of course, if you have your own garden, you can simply let him out into that.

DOG WALKING HELP?

Do you know someone who could occasionally help out with the care of your canine, be it for a few days in winter when you really can't get about outside at all, or if suffering from flu or some other unexpected bout of illness? Under these circumstances, would you always have to rely on commercial kennels?

In a household where there are also able-bodied family members, these disruptions to normal service can be dealt with easily enough. But every day that you can't go out means finding other people to walk your dog.

To cover any emergencies

that may arise, organize some neighbours, friends, relations or school children who can help out. It's best to have at least twice as many people as you think you'll need, because experience has shown that, in spite of promising otherwise, people can turn out to be less than reliable!

DIRT, ETC

Keeping a dog means more dirt will make its way into your house, partly because you bring it in yourself on your clothes and your wheelchair or scooter, and partly because a dog will bring it in – and spread it around pretty effectively! In addition, depending on what sort of dog you have, your entire household could be covered in dog hair after a few days.

In your personal living space, dirt is only *your* problem, but in any communal areas such as hallways, it may cause a great deal of annoyance. To prevent this, get yourself a floor mop which you can use easily from a wheelchair, and keep it somewhere close to hand so that you can immediately mop up the water outside your door that will drip from your dog and wheelchair or scooter whilst you rummage for your house key.

After switching to your indoor wheelchair or rollator, clean the area where you change and store the chair/scooter so that you don't spread dirt further into your living area. There's no point cleaning the wheelchair as it will be just as dirty again after the next walk!

With a little forethought, it's easy enough to clean up any doggy accidents, large or small, just by keeping a cleaning bucket, cloths, and disinfectant somewhere easily accessible in your living area, so that you can clear up a pile of poo without having to roll your wheelchair through it first!

GENERAL ISSUES

Before you get a dog, consider (and then arrange) insurance, find a (good) veterinary practice that you can get to without any help, and sort out the provision of food/bowls/ harnesses/bedding, etc, for your new companion. Many pet shops will make home deliveries for a small fee, although you may have to go and ask at the counter first. A medium-sized dog – depending on the type of food and his level of activity – will need about 20kg of food a month.

Will your dog mean enough to you to be worth all the outlay? A German Shepherd will cost about 65 a month, but this will mean shopping around for good deals, but remember that your four-legged friend needs to stay healthy all the time! If you like going on holiday and travelling the world, ridiculous international restrictions make this unnecessarily cumbersome with a dog. Would you prefer to spend your evenings in the pub rather than taking your dog for a walk in the woods? Does the breed of your dog mean that, by law, he will have to be on a lead or wear a muzzle all the time when you are out and about in public? If you belong to a sports club, consider whether you have the spare time and energy that a dog will require. Are you prepared to give up hobbies you enjoy for a dog?

In short, does a dog really fit with your current interests and lifestyle?

For a mobility-impaired person who hasn't yet got to grips with his own capabilities and options, the much celebrated idea of 'the courage to get

his own dog' will, at best, turn out to be a wilfully bad decision. Having your own dog can improve your quality of life and your health, which is why I'm deliberately not encouraging anyone to actually get a dog, but instead rather to carefully consider from all angles the feasibility of your situation with regard to welcoming a dog into your home – and your life …

🐕 Equipment

The mobility-impaired dog owner may need to acquire quite a range of equipment – wheelchair accessories, clothing, and a few things for the dog – before he is properly prepared to exercise his dog in all weathers.

THE WHEELCHAIR/SCOOTER FLEET

It's highly likely that, as a dog owner, you won't be able to get by with just the one wheelchair for outdoor use, given how much you are going to be doing. You will need a sturdy and high

The hand cycle: equipped for a two week break from civilisation.

quality set of wheels, and, preferably, a back-up replacement for when your main wheelchair is out of action. As a dog owner, you can't wait several days for a temporary replacement wheelchair, because of the need to be out and about at all times. Bear in mind the cost of a decent wheelchair; is it likely that your medical insurance provider will pay for more than one each for indoor and outdoor use?

Check also whether a wheelchair provided by an insurance company can be used to take out your dog, as it may be that it can only be used for 'essential shopping trips,' which would not include outings related to hobbies and leisure pursuits. In the event of an accident resulting in damage to the chair, the insurance company might not cover the costs of repair and you would have to meet these yourself.

You may be able to do without a backup wheelchair if you have the skills to provisionally fix a fault yourself.

To give medium- to large-sized dogs the amount of exercise they ideally need, you could use a racing wheelchair, or, even better, a hand cycle that you can attach to your usual wheelchair.

I have settled on the combination of a hand cycle and a conventional wheelchair. When I take my dog out for a quick pee early in the morning, I use the wheelchair, but, for a walk lasting several hours, there's no better piece of equipment than a hand cycle attached to a wheelchair.

A cushion for the chair, a waterproof cushion for wet days, a rucksack to carry all your bits and pieces in, puncture kit and tools for undertaking any repairs when

All-weather gear for the active, wheelchair- or scooter-using dog owner.

you are out – these are all items you will already have if you are used to spending time outdoors, but if this is a new experience for you, you'll probably have to buy them. During the course of a year, you will probably end up doing a third of all your dog walks in the dark, so will need powered reflectors. For paths through fields, safe passage in winter on ice and snow, and to ensure that you can find the edge of the kerb when it is hidden under snow, you will need a reasonably-sized and quite powerful spotlight and a battery, which should be fitted to the wheelchair or scooter. These are all items that the average wheelchair/ scooter user has no need for, because he will be sitting at home, warm and dry, and maybe dreaming of having his own dog.

Skilful wheelchair/scooter technique is at least as important as strength and stamina. In some situations, skill will help you negotiate a tricky situation, whereas going at it like a bull in a china shop may mean you simply become stuck, or literally hit the deck when your chair turns over. Have you already had enough experience with your wheelchair or scooter to take your dog on country tracks through fields and woods, and also some off-road, cross-country routes?

CLOTHING

Unfortunately, many wheelchair/ scooter users only go out when the weather is nice, but, as a dog owner, you will have to go out whatever the

Equipped for tour temperatures of minus 15 degrees C – bank robbery also an option ...

weather. An umbrella and a cagoule from the supermarket won't be of any use to you, as you won't be able to hold the umbrella and basic clothing won't keep you warm or dry.

A system of layers is the most practical clothing arrangement, especially for anyone with restricted mobility.

In terms of outer wear, choose high quality, breathable, all-weather clothing for the summer. For incessant rain, an outfit made of non-breathable, waterproof material is a must, as even the highest quality material won't dry properly after several rainy days in a row. Waterproof cyclist galoshes will keep your feet dry in stormy showers, and you'll also need special, non-slip gloves, sturdy, insulated and waterproof footwear to protect your immobile feet, as well as possibly insulated trousers with insulated knee pads for when it's really cold.

If you need to have a complete change of clothes – including your underwear – after every walk, this isn't going to do you much good in the long term. In summer, it only takes a few seconds to change a sweaty t-shirt, but layers of winter clothing mean it will take you several minutes to get down to basics! It's worth getting some good quality

thermal underwear that wicks moisture away to the outside whilst staying dry.

All-in-one trousers with a lining, knee protectors, and a rainproof outer layer may seem like a good idea, but they require more of an effort than wearing fleece long johns with thin thermal trousers over them, and the option of waterproof trousers as a third layer. You will usually not need the latter, but take them with you in your rucksack just in case. You can wear the fleece trousers all day around the house, and put on the thermal trousers before you go out. The all-in-one trousers are never really quite right for any weather conditions, and you always have to change completely if you have been wearing them.

Foot-warmers are a necessary piece of equipment; in really cold temperatures, even the best boots can't prevent immobile feet from getting extremely cold, which can result in a urinary tract or kidney infection that will weaken your whole body. Some kind of heating device is the answer here; professional solutions to this problem include heated socks or insoles, which are available from specialist shops.

Next to wheelchairs, clothing is the most expensive element of your equipment. A complete outfit, like that detailed above, will set you

Get some electric foot-warmers for your boots in winter, but be sensible!

back about ●850, if you shop around. But bear in mind that cheap goods from a department store will be soaked through after you've been out in the rain for just two minutes: by the evening, you will be in hospital with pneumonia; two days later, you will be lying in a coma in intensive care. Your mother will cry. Your dog will howl. An able-bodied person can take an umbrella as protection if his clothing turns out to be unsuitable; not an option for the mobility-impaired who needs practical apparel from the start. In order to cater for his additional physical requirements, this gear is higher quality and therefore more expensive.

SPECIAL EQUIPMENT FOR YOUR FOUR—LEGGED FRIEND

In addition to the bits and pieces that the owner needs to successfully get by, it is also necessary to purchase a few accessories for your dog.

Necessities

Harness, etc, food bowl, water bowl

(also portable versions), a bed, a few toys (more about this later); a brush. You don't need any more than this. It may be necessary to trim claws but I personally think that cleaning a dog's teeth is nonsensical; a dog that is properly fed generally does not suffer from any serious dental problems. What is and is not necessary will become obvious once you start living together.

In terms of nutrition and medical care, seek advice from the same places and people as every other dog owner. Feed your dog on complete dog food from a specialist shop, not on cheap rubbish from a discount store, or cook your own meat and mix with vegetables, paste or rice. Your supplier will give you advice as to which food is most suitable for your dog's needs. When you take your dog for his first vaccinations and worming, the vet will give you information about potential medical requirements and other aspects of caring responsibly for your dog. After this, you can proceed on the basis of 'everything will be revealed in time.'

"Your dog's teeth should be free of plaque," says the vet. Instead of a toothbrush, Falco, the stray, cleans his teeth with stones ...

The lead problem

In my opinion, no properly trained dog needs a lead. As a wheelchair/scooter user, you can't stop a big dog anyway if he decides to take off. If you are out and about in a conventional wheelchair, a dog on a lead will impair your balance. Whilst you are propelling the chair, you can't hold the lead in your hand, and most of the dog lead holders intended for cyclists won't work with most wheelchairs – quite aside from the fact that it's not permissible to fit them to a chair that has been provided by a medical insurance company. Even if you manage to improvise, as your forward propulsion occurs in fits and starts, it will mean that the lead jolts about, because it's never completely taut until you really get some speed up. If the dog and the wheelchair user get too close to each other, either the dog trips over the lead or it becomes tangled in the wheelchair. This effect cannot even be completely avoided on significantly steadier journeys using a hand cycle.

In short, then, if your dog isn't at the very least fairly well trained, you're going to have problems with a wheelchair/scooter and a lead. And for a dog which has learnt to run alongside a wheel, attaching it to a mechanical lead is just superfluous nonsense.

However, the law says that dogs must be on a lead. No matter what you want to do, you need a lead (and obviously a collar as well), even if you can't use it from a wheelchair without endangering yourself, the dog, and

Dog harness with and without lights.

everyone else. I've travelled tens of thousands of miles with dozens of dogs and never had an accident – or used a lead. It works. But the law sees it somewhat differently …

Here are a few tips to help you comply with any legal obligation to put your dog on a lead, without killing yourself and your dog on the first outing.

You can purchase a simple harness from a pet shop with a hand-length section running parallel to the spine of the dog. On a German Shepherd or a Golden Retriever, this 'handle' will be at a comfortable height for you to hold, which means that you can travel short distances safely, but can quickly let go of the dog if needed. Another option, favoured by Dogs for the Disabled when training people with their assistance dogs, is to use a lead that has velcro attached to the inside of the lead loop, which will then snugly attach around the upper arm (which tends not to move as energetically as the hand when self-propelling) of the wheelchair user, thus keeping the lead up and away from the wheels. The most suitable equipment for actual lead use is an extending

How the harness should be worn, with a badge that provides ownership/contact details.

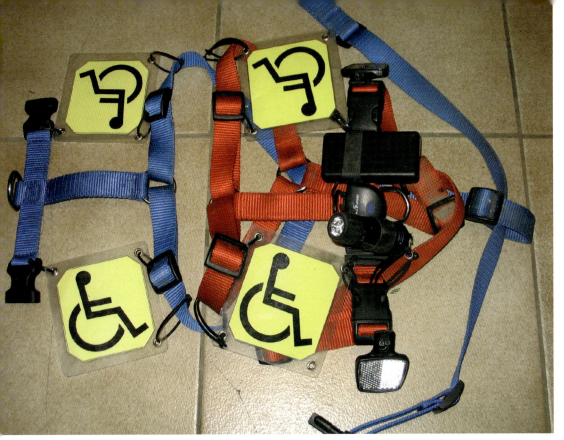

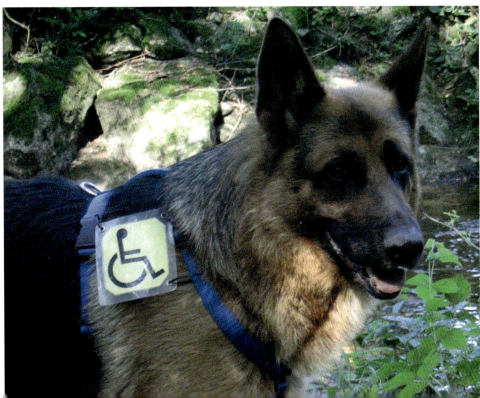

Canine control without a lead.

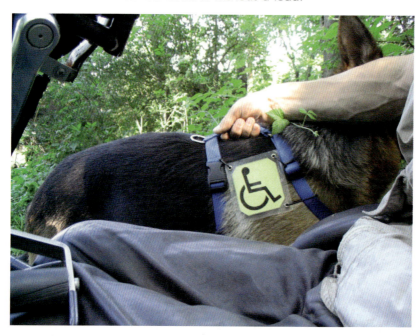

user's upper body with an easily accessible karabiner clip. By securing the handle with a panic clip from an equestrian equipment supplier, which opens when put under pressure, you also retrain your own reflex response from 'grip the wheelchair' to 'let go of the dog,' which may help prevent a fall.

Run the rope diagonally from one side of your neck under the opposite arm. Keep the extending lead unlocked and flexible, which allows your dog to run freely beside you within a specified zone, without getting stuck in narrow gaps lead, the handle of which should be secured to a thick mountaineering rope, secured around the wheelchair between the wheelchair and an obstacle. He will be aware that

Simplified version of lead attachment which is more adaptable – though just as dangerous if things go wrong ...

Attachment of the lead to the wheelchair user in this way can be extremely dangerous, for obvious reasons.

he is on the lead and cannot run wherever he wants. The spring in the lead compensates for the variable propulsion speed to a certain extent – your dog can walk at a constant pace with only intermittent, slight tugs on his harness. If he takes off, however, when the lead reaches its full extent, he could pull you out of the wheelchair/off the scooter and onto the road (if you don't manage to release the panic clip in time, which is what usually happens, because you have both hands on the wheels or handlebars).

An extending lead set to about 1.5 metres, with the heavy handgrip lying loose in your lap, will not slip down, but also will not stop your dog in an emergency. It reassures passers-by, and complies with the stipulation for having your dog on a lead – to all intents, at least. If the dog does not walk in exemplary fashion right next to the wheelchair or scooter, the lead may still get tangled, but you are not endangered if your dog decides to take off.

It would perhaps be possible to fit a lead holder meant for bicycles to the wheelchair, hand cycle or scooter so that your dog can walk beside you, firmly secured. However, this makes you far too wide to pass on most paths and through most doors; nor will you be able to use many lifts, and will get stuck at the supermarket checkout. Should your dog stop suddenly, or try to take off to the side, he may still pull the wheelchair into the path of moving traffic, just as he would if he were secured by any other type of fixed connection to either owner or mobility aide.

Anyone who uses an electric wheelchair only will not have any of these problems. An electric wheelchair user always has one hand free for the lead, and enough weight and stability to be able to hold even the largest dog. But anyone who uses hand-propelled techniques to resolve the issues presented by steps and terraces knows that the wheelchair user generally moves in a way that involves turning, accelerating, stopping and tilting, and means that no dog on a lead could move fast enough to accommodate this. In addition, these are manoeuvres during which the wheelchair user cannot have anything else affecting his balance.

All this aside, you should ensure that you have the following to hand. A collar and an identity tag (required by law); a harness; and then, of course, the (extending) lead. And a chew-resistant cord. Dogs will only take seconds to chew through mountaineering rope the thickness of your thumb in order to follow you into the supermarket if they don't like waiting outside alone.

Optional extras

If you can't avoid train travel, be aware that in some countries (Germany, for example), all dogs must wear a muzzle and be on a lead to travel this way.

Attach the lead to a chest harness rather than a collar for the first few times that you use trains, buses

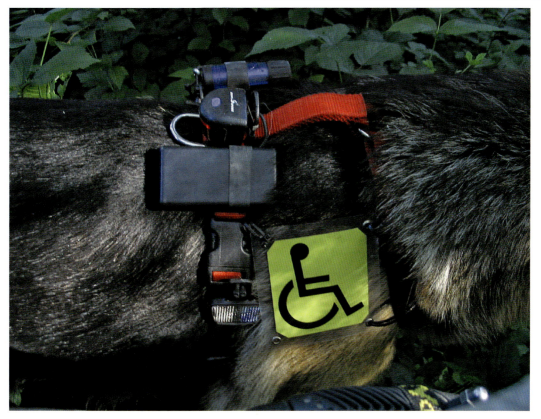

Lights for dark mornings and evenings. Brilliant white lights pointing forwards, red lights pointing backwards, plus battery pack and side reflectors.

and similar vehicles, until your dog has got used to the experience; he can't back out of a harness if he is nervous. In fact, it's preferable, and kinder, to always attach the lead to the harness, rather than the collar.

I do not regard scented pheromone collars – or, the crueller alternative, electronic collars – as necessary. I also don't believe you need a dog whistle or a clicker.

If your dog has a reflective safety jacket or a collar with a flashing light on it – or, even better, a harness with a light on the front and a red rear light at the back, as collars can disappear under thick fur – he becomes a visible obstacle. At the time of year when it gets dark early, as a wheelchair or scooter user you can no longer travel muddy, snowy, cross-country paths, and are therefore often restricted to the road.

Get a cover for your dog that you can throw over him before you go through the main entrance into your building. This ensures that other tenants will not be irritated by dirt sprays in the hallway when he

... and folded up very small, ready for packing.

Travel food and water bowl in use ...

Paw 'bootees' which are designed to protect sound paws on long tours and rough ground, but are also very useful for protecting injured paws (and overleaf).

These look like beanie hats, can be rolled up to the size of a tennis ball, are suitable for every type of food, and can hold water for several hours.

It's also sensible to use special paw protectors, which you put on your dog before his paws show signs of wear and tear, on a dog whose capabilities you are not yet sure about, or when you are going on an exceptionally long hike. I always carry them with me, but have never yet had to use them on my own dog. What counts is thorough knowledge of your animal and making sure that you take sensible precautions in terms of emergency supplies.

shakes. From outdoor equipment shops you can buy lightweight rucksack covers that fold up into fist-sized packages, which are big enough to cover a German Shepherd.

For longer hikes and holidays, it also makes sense to buy foldable, lightweight food and drink bowls.

Furthermore, everyone will create their own domestic first aid kit as they go along, which may include some ointment for paws that become

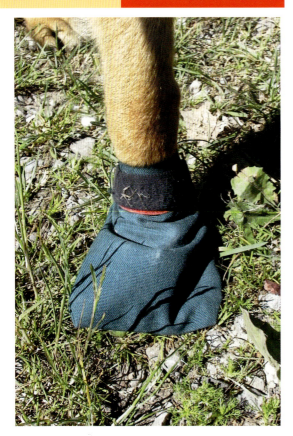

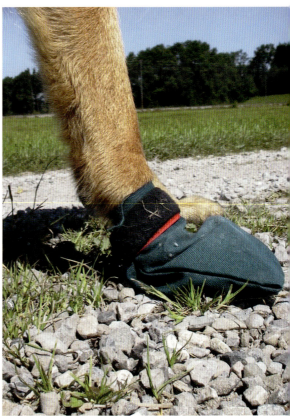

Checkmate?

extra sensitive in winter, flea or mite powder, ointment for ear mites, a thermometer, and (indispensable) a special tick-removing tool that ensures all of the creature is removed,without leaving the head behind (which can result in infection).

Toys

Opinions differ greatly about toys. Some people think that a dog with no toys is completely deprived – and it is true to say that it is important for a dog to have mental as well as physical exercise and stimulation – but my dog ignores toys. He's never used the chess computer, just chewed it, and is happy when he can have a nice, long, undisturbed sleep when he gets home. At night, he is busy sleeping and dreaming. When we are outside, we are on the go. During breaks on walks, every dog will find enough interesting things in the great outdoors to play with.

Observe for yourself what your dog

Come on; throw the stone instead of just sitting around like that!

accepts and uses to occupy himself. The souvenir brought back from the forest is often far more interesting than some plastic thing from a factory.

But if you must buy him toys, initially, get a squeaky toy and a chewy ring. Dig out an old ball from somewhere, then base your decision on whether or not to get more on your dog's reaction to this. Playing with other members of his species or with the human species is significantly more important to a dog than any boring game by himself with some random objects.

Dog toys for outdoors are near enough impossible for the mobility-impaired person to use. It makes more sense to use natural bits and pieces that your dog finds by the side of the path. Untrained dogs will always leave their toy somewhere – usually where the wheelchair user cannot reach — and the toy will be lost.

Visit Hubble and Hattie on the web: www.hubbleandhattie.com and www.hubbleandhattie.blogspot.com
Details of all books • New book news • Special offers

The dog

Not only do you need to be fit to be an owner, but the dog you choose must also be a good match for you, which is why it is worth taking some time to think about what breeds and sizes might be the most suitable.

POSSIBLE BREEDS FOR THE MOBILITY–IMPAIRED DOG OWNER

It is possible. of course, for a wheelchair or scooter user to own virtually any breed of dog, but what is needed, first and foremost, is a well trained dog, which can cope with a degree of off-lead freedom, since this will be beneficial to both parties.

Dogs bred for hunting are doubtful candidates; if you simply have to have a Munsterlander, a Setter or a Weimaraner, don't be surprised when the inevitable happens if you take him off-lead through the woods! On the other hand, Retrievers, like the Golden Retriever or Labrador, which have no interest in rushing around killing things but just fetch what has already been killed, are very well suited. Huskies will demand too much of you physically, whilst anyone who is mobility-impaired will never be able to take full advantage of the intelligence and work ethic of the Border Collie. In both cases, the mismatch will result in an unhappy animal.

If you also take into account the prejudices of our fellow human beings when choosing your four-legged friend – German Shepherds are aggressive fighters, Golden Retrievers are soft teddy bears, all Terriers are yappy – there aren't many breeds left to choose from.

A big dog needs a great deal of skilled assertiveness from his owner. If you and he have a falling out, dogs the size of a German Shepherd (and bigger) are quite capable of dragging you down the road at the end of a lead. Which is why someone in a chair, who is not necessarily capable of physically reining in a dog, requires much more experience than an able-bodied person who, if the worst comes to the worst, can resort to physical force. Do you have enough theoretical and practical experience with dogs to be sure that your chosen companion will definitely and unquestioningly do what he is told?

Finally, there is the question of

Standard dog harness with home-made wheelchair badges which carry contact information on the back, in case the dog should become lost.

how much time do you want to spend grooming your dog? I don't brush my German Shepherd every day, but then he doesn't bring very much dirt into the flat on his coat or his paws. On the other hand, a Golden Retriever or Old English Sheepdog with their fulsome coats, do need regular grooming. And, of course, brushing the coat is of benefit to your dog also, so should be done on a regular basis.

Dog size and ability
More important than breed is the dog's size and ability.

What is the extent of your mobility? If you normally travel at a steady, average walking pace, you should avoid large dogs who like lots of brisk walking; a dog the size of a Dachshund would be a better fit for you. Collies, German Shepherds and Retrievers are breeds that will not be hard work for the average wheelchair/hand cycle/scooter user covering longer distances. The same applies to crossbreeds of these and other breeds. Some medium-size crossbreeds, such as Labrador and Bernese Mountain Dog crosses, have shown themselves to be very capable walkers.

Small breeds are out of the question for active wheelchair/scooter users and hand cyclists: there's no point getting a Yorkshire Terrier, a Dachshund, Chihuahua, Spitz, or Miniature Poodle, unless you intend taking him for a walk in your rucksack!

On the other hand, all of the sled dog breeds will prove too much for the average wheelchair/scooter user: a 10 mile/15 kilometre walk is just a warm-up for a Husky. Because the typical characteristics of a sled dog are usually retained when they are crossbred, many owners will find it impossible to cope with even a Husky cross.

The active wheelchair user with a hand cycle is able to give his dog more exercise than someone on foot. He can maintain a steady speed of around 8mph/12kph, which is ideal

Ferro takes the chance to rest in a shady forest. Camping tours that last several days are tiring, even for the trained dog.

for medium-sized and larger dogs. The wheelchair user's dog will not be able to complain about a lack of exercise, although he might complain about not being allowed to run free with his owner in the great outdoors. Your dog should indeed be allowed to run free during off-lead training, with you accompanying him along the nearest pathways.

There's one thing you should remember in relation to size and choosing your dog. In the event of a biting incident, the owner of a big dog will always get the blame, no matter what may have led to the incident. A big dog leaves the biggest marks, and will therefore be considered a dangerous animal, even if he had been thoroughly teased and provoked beforehand. People in general consider a bite from a large dog to be much more serious than a bite from a small one. Nevertheless, the wheelchair/scooter user who wants his dog with him all the time – to take shopping in town, rambling and swimming – will be best served by one that is medium-to-large in size.

DON'T COMPROMISE

In spite of all of these considerations, don't compromise. Don't get a medium-sized mongrel when you'd really rather have a Newfoundland. Your dog will be with you all day, every day, for the next ten to fifteen years. You will be investing a lot of money, time, effort and care, maybe rearranging your life completely to accommodate him, and you won't want to do this for a 'compromise' dog. Take the time to think over what you really want, and what is really possible for you, taking into account your financial, physical and domestic circumstances, and how you can modify these to enable you to get the dog that you want. Never let pity lead you to adopt a dog from a rescue centre that you are not 100 per cent sure of. And don't take the sweet little puppy home just so "The poor thing will have a good life now." The dog you get as a compromise, or the one you adopt because you feel sorry for it, may become impossible to keep, and you will both end up miserable if you have to rehome him …

SELECTION AND PURCHASE

All animal refuges and dogs' homes will curse me when they read this, but the fact is that using a wheelchair or other mobility aide restricts certain aspects of dog training. This is why it is significantly more advantageous to go to a responsible, reputable breeder to find a puppy or adolescent dog that is well socialised with people and other dogs, and has papers documenting his healthy status, than opting to go to the animal refuge for a sweet, but maybe poorly mongrel with no information about his level of training or possible behavioural defects, which may make it impossible for a wheelchair user to cope with him.

With a dog from a breeder, wait until practically all of the puppies have been chosen. The most reserved (not the shyest or the most timid) animal – which is usually the last one left – is the one that you can allow a lot of freedom without any preparatory work, as he is unlikely to react aggressively, and his cautious nature will present far fewer problems than that of a more self-assured, dominant dog. These animals are often rejected by the 'well-informed' prospective dog owner, as most people, even when choosing a Golden Retriever as their family pet, will opt for the animal with a strong character, even though this means that the owner will need to be more assertive.

When making your purchase, stress the benefits that the dog will enjoy when he comes to live with you: long walks, because you have a lot of leisure time; company most of the time because you either don't work, or you work from home. Some people hesitate to sell a dog to a wheelchair user; my local animal refuge refused to let me have a dog, despite my fifteen years of experience with them, so I went to a breeder …

THE RIGHT TIME TO GET A DOG, AND THE AGE OF THE DOG

The training methods I recommend here as advantageous for wheelchair/scooter users can be applied with the same degree of success with puppies, young adult or adult dogs. They have always proved effective with dogs of between one and six years of age, regardless of what the dog has previously experienced or suffered. The mobility-impaired dog owner does not necessarily need to get a puppy in order to ensure that the dog learns to focus on him to the extent that is necessary, but you should probably do your best to avoid having your first experience of training and owning a dog with a badly-behaved animal that came from a dubious source.

Give careful consideration to whether you can actually manage puppy training. You can't take a puppy for long walks; the best you can do is take him out in a rucksack when he needs to do his business, and – given the complications of life in a wheelchair – by the time you've finally got him house-trained, you may be completely fed-up with the whole idea of dog ownership. For puppy training, you need to have the use of a small garden at the very least, which no one else uses or has any say about. It is highly advantageous if you have an able-bodied person in your household who can share the burden of the two hourly walks over the first few weeks, and who can take charge of cleaning up the accidents that will inevitably occur in the house during this time.

Consider not just the age of the dog but the time of year when you get him. It is preferable to do this in early spring, as every day the weather is getting warmer and drier, and more country tracks will become passable with a wheelchair or a scooter. Soon you will be able to tackle some short cross-country stretches, and you will have become an experienced team by the time the bad weather sets in in autumn, and certainly by the tiresome winter season. At that point, you will be able to concentrate fully on the difficulties presented by the weather, as training and the getting-to-know each other phase have already been dealt with.

SHOULD YOU HAVE YOUR OWN DOG OR JUST BORROW ONE?

Walking a dog safely, given the restrictions imposed by using a wheelchair/scooter, and controlling an animal that hasn't been trained in line with your requirements necessitates a fair degree of experience. But how can a wheelchair user acquire this, other than by having his own dog? One solution could be to borrow a dog; perhaps looking after one when the owner is at work. The dog will have company and get extra exercise that the owner isn't able to give him, and this may help you get an idea of the sort of problems you might experience, allow you to explore in practice whether dog ownership is really for you, and if you are ready to put in the work that having your own dog entails.

Don't, whatever you do, rush out and get a dog, realise after a few days that you have no control over the situation, either at home or out and about, and only then think about researching training and behaviour. Dog ownership is no fun at all under these circumstances – for the dog or you!

When I was starting out on the dog ownership project, a borrowed dog encouraged me to refine my wheelchair technique and to try cross-country expeditions and walks in the woods. He encouraged me to put together a fleet of wheelchairs and get myself special, all-weather clothing suitable for keeping a wheelchair user comfortable in temperatures ranging from plus 30 to minus 20 degrees. If, at this point, however, I had had to look after the dog all year round all the time, I would have found it too much and it would soon have become very unenjoyable.

THE 'ASSISTANCE DOG'

The general public often closely associates the key word 'disabled' with the concept of an 'assistance dog.' I mentioned at the start that a dog in general does not help to rehabilitate you, but is, in fact, an encumbrance, and would like to qualify this statement to some extent.

For someone who has only recently become a wheelchair user, a dog should never be considered when contemplating and coming to terms with what life in a wheelchair will be like. Dog ownership necessitates having in place all the basic equipment that a mobility-impaired individual needs, as well as a certain level of stability in terms of state of health and mind. When you have reached that point, a dog can be the stimulus for accelerated rehabilitation; the motivation to explore remaining physical capabilities and to develop and therefore enhance them. In the beginning, you have to relearn so many things in your daily life that the newly mobility-impaired person who lives alone will find the additional demands of a dog completely overwhelming.

For this reason I suggest that you get a dog a year after you have been discharged from hospital at the earliest – and only then once you have done a very detailed analysis of your situation and capabilities. It takes this long to master the most critical wheelchair/scooter techniques, and you will have experienced a whole year of the changes to your body, and built up a serviceable amount of strength and stamina for the completely different movements now needed to get around. You will have slowly got to grips with it all and reached a point where life has resumed a degree of predictability. And now you would like to branch out a bit, which is where a dog can be a useful stimulus. Still keep in mind, however, that a dog represents a big commitment for several years, and not just in terms of how to organise your leisure time.

Having your own dog obliges you to be more active; in this respect, a dog can be said to take an active role in rehabilitation and prevention of ill-health!

Getting a dog means taking on a whole range of responsibilities. You have to get involved with another creature and shape its behaviour. You have to deal with this creature's needs, impulses and desires in order to reach some form of consensus with which both parties are happy to live. You have to get used to being flexible and ready to often alter your customary routine. Trying to fit a dog into your existing daily schedule is unlikely to be successful, and it is possible he will change or even render impracticable many of your favourite habits. All-in-all, you have to be prepared to trade-in physical and mental ease to achieve a really desirable relationship. In this respect, your four-legged friend certainly has a positive psychological effect which can also aid rehabilitation.

AN AMAZING RELATIONSHIP?

There's another myth that you shouldn't use as an excuse to make a hasty decision about acquiring your own dog: that a special connection exists between a disabled person and a dog!

However, the extreme closeness in the relationship between the wheelchair/scooter user and his companion, which is achieved purely through the fact that the former is always sitting down, is not to be sneezed at. You are always accessible to the dog – and that makes him happy. Because you can't physically tower over him, you inadvertently show that you have friendly intentions, and he likes that.

Once your dog is living with you, he quickly learns that his master provides reasonable protection from any assailant. A dog can hide quite nicely behind a wheelchair or a scooter. A disabled person can be, perhaps, more tolerant and tend to have more empathy; he has learnt to take graphic defects and extensive physical limitations into account, and can translate these experiences into dealing compassionately with a different species. The mature composure that you learn by having to deal with your own restricted mobility makes an important contribution to your relationship with an animal. Even an illness such as diabetes causes a person to meticulously observe tiny variations in his own behaviour and feelings, and these powers of analysis can be used in dealing with your surroundings, and any companion animal you may acquire, making it easier to read and understand your dog's behaviour. As the owner then manages to communicate more appropriate guidance, the dog has more confidence in him and understands him more easily.

This kind of same level communication between a disabled person and his dog is essentially the result of completely mundane factors. The disability itself plays much less of a role than to what extent it has shaped the individual; what you have learnt from your disability may have given you a special perception, but 'may' is the key word here, because you can also be completely destroyed by a disability without having learnt anything at all. So you can never rely on the premise "I'm disabled – it will all just fall into place for me," as nothing will just fall into place. Your disability means that you will have to give particularly careful consideration to many issues. The perfectly behaved German Shepherd who trots along beside his owner, stops willingly at the kerb and leads the wheelchair or scooter user across the road when there is a break in the traffic, is not like that by chance, but a product of the owner's work on himself and on that animal.

In tune and on the same wavelength.

THE BENEFITS OF DOG OWNERSHIP

The ways in which your life will be affected by owning a dog can be summarised in a few sentences. He will eat up all your household budget; make your house dirty; and force you to go outside several times a day, whatever the weather. He is the cause of arguments with the neighbours, and can lead to his owner rubbing everyone up the wrong way.

However, an animal-lover will not be concerned with how he will profit from the arrangement, and will get himself a dog in spite of these potential issues.

A dog can prevent his owner from undertaking possibly injurious and unhealthy short-term bursts of extreme activity; instead, inducing progressive exertion which improves physical fitness and the circulation, and helps stabilise your state of health.

A knock-on effect is that the impact of more major health issues, to which disabled people are often prone, is lessened due to overall improvement in health and fitness. Insomnia and other sleep disorders, which are often caused by the physical neglect of your own body, can be overcome without resorting to medication or psychiatry. And children who, instead of spending all their free time fighting monsters on the computer, go out on their bikes with the dog to go swimming in the river, are much less likely to end up disturbed, having learnt from their earliest years about give and take.

They also tend to act more on their own initiative, and are not already overweight by the time they are in junior school.

These are just a few of the many ways in which the dog contributes to keeping us in good health, preventing many diseases of modern civilization.

Regular extended exercise is proven to help with weight reduction, and stabilises the metabolism where metabolic deficiencies exist.

Dogs are stress-relievers, and lower blood pressure and the proportion of certain harmful substance in the blood, thereby reducing the risk of heart attacks and strokes – as demonstrated by numerous medical studies.

In addition, a disabled person who is at risk of becoming socially isolated will find that his four-legged friend forces him to participate in life outside his own four walls.

And my personal insights after my years of dog ownership? My health is now stable, and I am no longer prey to the illnesses that used to regularly prevent me leaving the house.

Typical complaints for those suffering from paralysis, such as urinary tract infections, muscular tension or neuralgia, improved significantly or completely disappeared. My dog didn't induce me to walk – although sometimes I would have given anything to be able to jump up and kick him up the backside – but he introduced me to a way of life which has resulted in a huge improvement in my physical condition.

Words are not necessary; the picture says it all …

AND, AS AN ADDED BONUS: PSYCHOLOGICAL BENEFITS

The following section should be read with a pinch of salt, because it's the tale of somebody who was, to a certain extent, sick in the head, who details his symptoms and then declares them cured. Nevertheless, I would ask you to humour me through the next few sentences. It gets a little more straightforward again afterwards …

In spite of all the problems, the effort necessary to satisfy legal requirements, and inter-personal hostilities, after about six months of having my own dog I began to notice all kinds of positive psychological effects. I was falling asleep quickly at night again for the first time in many years, no longer spending hours tossing and turning sleeplessly, and waking every morning drenched in sweat with the thought "Oh God, yet another shitty day to get through!"

Previously, I had always known how to keep busy, but the emotional impetus was missing. Suddenly, it was back. Once again, I could feel that mild, warm weather was something positive. I stopped seeing problems as stressful pressures, and changed my attitude to one of sitting back and letting the problems come to me, so that I could beat them to a pulp. It only became clear to me at this point exactly how much at sea my emotional state had been.

The politician, who would far rather see the proles going to work than loafing around with dogs, might claim that I could have achieved the same effect by having a career – but I would dare to question that. The psychologist, who prefers to see friendships with animals as inferior, might object by saying that a sensible friendship with a human would have produced even more positive effects. I would doubt that too, as this assumption makes no allowance for all kinds of inalterable factors.

I have to say that it is certainly not the case that someone who is depressed will automatically become happier just because he gets a dog. But, whatever you actively make of your relationship with the animal, I believe that, at some point, it will have a positive effect on you. You can't just sit there passively and wait for it to happen, however, as then the dog will just become an obligation that is forcing you into activity, an additional pressure that is likely to make you more unhappy. In order to have a mutually beneficial relationship with your dog, in the first instance you need to be ready to make sacrifices, have a certain degree of empathy, and all kinds of basic knowledge to be able to create the basis of a relationship with which you can work. Anyone who tries to build a relationship for which he hasn't done the groundwork is on a hiding to nothing. And anyone who only does the groundwork so that he can exploit it later, will – at least in terms of his relationship with the animal – give up in frustration before getting to enjoy the fruits of his labours. The rule of thumb is that whatever you invest in sharing your life with a dog, you will get back a hundred times over.

Visit Hubble and Hattie on the web: www.hubbleandhattie.com and www.hubbleandhattie.blogspot.com
Details of all books • New book news • Special offers

Dog training for the mobility-impaired

Since I have been dependent on a wheelchair to get around, I have made every effort to use skilful guidance to ensure that my dog behaves in a way that suits my requirements.

There are numerous ways to train a dog appropriately. Generally, however, these do not even touch on the issues which are of most importance to the mobility-impaired dog owner – the maintenance of independent behaviour when the dog is off the lead, and abandoning the use of sanctions which are not compatible with being in a chair or on a scooter. A method of training can only be said to be compatible with wheelchair/scooter use if the end result is a dog that is suitable for a wheelchair user: of course, the method must also be suitable for the wheelchair user to apply.

THE BASICS OF DOG TRAINING

Any training must be adapted to suit the character and abilities of your dog. and the first task is to discover the channels of communication that work best for him. These can be audible (verbal commands), visual (gestures), physical (restraining,

stroking), or scent-based (smell). Decide what information you want to impart through these channels, and ask yourself: how do I talk to my dog?

BEHAVIOURAL FUNDAMENTALS: THE DOG'S CHARACTER

It is also important to closely study the behaviour of the trainee. Training and obedience are contrary to the dog's natural desire to move up the pecking order, although this does not mean that you have to act like a tyrant to remain master of the situation. Much more effective is demonstrating experience and ability, because dogs are keen to align themselves with someone who knows what's what.

Your relationship with your dog is not static. A well trained dog will still try to jostle for position. It is important, therefore, to treat him as an individual, otherwise he will try to usurp your dominant role in the relationship, eventually becoming more and more difficult to manage.

LEARNING BEHAVIOUR

Every intelligent being depends on the capacity to learn in order to survive and flourish in his particular environment. An advanced natural learning ability is thus an integral part of every dog, and can be harnessed by natural or artificial means.

Dogs are not stupid, and numerous examples exist which demonstrate how intelligent they are. They can perform complex activities, remember what they have learned surprisingly well, and learn how to distinguish between very small details.

Getting a dog to do anything requires some form of stimulus or motivation. Negative reinforcement, or learning through punishment, has a destructive influence on the dog, creates detachment, and is often not productive.

Learning through positive reinforcement – using food as a reward – usually facilitates a more direct and less destructive route to achieving your objectives, and is a far kinder and more respectful approach. In addition, the dog does not live in constant fear but looks forward to experiencing something positive.

Human teaching skills

A number of basic principles make it possible for a dog to learn.

Firstly, every lesson must be broken down into small, easily understood steps and repeated several times. The dog must first understand what's required and then actively choose to do it. Each command must be perfectly clear, and apply to a single action only.

A methodical approach is not only necessary during training, but must also be strictly maintained in your life together – at least as far as the most important commands are concerned. Otherwise, your dog will gradually disassociate the commands with the desired action and the connection will become more and more tenuous.

In all of this, the owner must be aware of his dog's abilities. Training can be significantly simplified if the teacher uses gestures and sounds that the dog naturally understands, supplemented by unambiguous human gestures and facial expressions. Give top priority to narrowing the huge gap between what interests a human and what interests a dog. When doing this, don't ignore what your dog wants, but learn to accept the nature of the beast. Don't stop your four-legged friend from communicating; react to what he says in the same way as you expect him to react to you. That way, you are treating him like a companion and he will be much more comfortable with you than a dog which is in a tyrannically imposed relationship. However, you should deal with any undesirable behaviour immediately rather than waiting until later when there may be no option but to adopt a much tougher approach. Remaining relaxed while you are instructing your dog will help make him more alert and responsive to your needs.

Design every learning situation in such a way that your dog is able to recognize that chastisement happens as a natural consequence of events, rather than something you have deliberately engineered. Let your dog know that your commands are for his own protection, and nothing else. Do not insist that your dog learns a detailed list of commands but have just a small number of useful instructions.

Get your dog used to your way of doing things through steady and regular reinforcement, but do not try to change his character completely. Work on minimizing unacceptable character traits gradually over time. Insist on behaviour that is appropriate, even though what you are looking for might not be immediately obvious. Forceful intervention – especially when attempted by the layman – holds enormous dangers, and can turn a placid dog into an aggressive biter. Make only those changes that are really necessary.

Training your dog like this will shape him into a reliable companion, and a true and faithful friend. If you take this general approach, you will create a verbal and emotional connection to your dog that is much more effective and secure than any lead you buy from the pet shop, yet is much easier to use and a lot more flexible.

SOME DIFFERENCES IN TRAINING AND CONTROL

A dog belonging to a wheelchair or scooter user must be trained for off-lead freedom right from the start, but he should never be allowed to extend the bounds of this in an arbitrary manner. One of the most important training objectives for the independent wheelchair user who wants to use a manually-operated wheelchair (and so therefore has to use his hands to propel himself) to undertake expeditions with his dog, has to be a peaceable dog which will not aggressively bother either people or other animals.

Enabling the dog to have this degree of freedom necessitates a strong bond with the owner. However, the dog must be capable of taking himself off on command to explore places that he cannot investigate with his owner because of the latter's restricted mobility.

Training must be based on positive reinforcement with no mutual trials of strength: an animal which, for the purposes of controlling it, constantly has to be restrained in training or thereafter, is of no use to the wheelchair or scooter user.

FRIENDLINESS HAS TO BE TAUGHT

If you want a friendly dog, be a friend to him first, but be a guiding friend rather than a dictatorial tyrant, which will result in a servile companion with no initiative or will of his own. So forget any training scheme based on subordination. And forget any ideas about oppressive training. All a dog needs is for his natural self-assurance to be (kindly) reined in from time to time.

For the most part, you don't need to get involved in your dog's contact with other dogs you may meet, as long as the other dog owner is okay with this and the situation doesn't degenerate into snapping and biting. Protect your dog from any aggression directed at him, and reprimand him if he tries to play the part of dominant aggressor. If you take hold of the scruff of his neck and hold him to the ground, it's not going to hurt him, but will be far more humbling for him than being whacked, which is a typically human way of expressing anger. However, it should only be necessary to do this in extreme cases, and not used as a regular chastisement.

Act immediately to check his behaviour the first time that you notice your dog trying to chase joggers or cyclists, or children that he wants to play with – they will inevitably fall over and then you will be in trouble, even though there was no malign intention behind his behaviour. Only if you are persistently firm in all areas will you end up with an animal that you can really trust off the lead.

Timely intervention should only briefly disturb the harmony of your relationship with your dog; after a few minutes, be just as friendly as if nothing bad had happened. This is the language that the dog understands.

OFF THE LEAD MUST BE TAUGHT

The basic prerequisite for off-lead walking is a friendly but reserved dog. You need to build the self-confidence of a timid, insecure dog before you can let him off the lead,

otherwise he will just run under the next car in a panic or suffer from nervous aggression. And you will need to check the behaviour of a dog with aggressive tendencies before letting him off the lead.

Being off the lead cannot mean riotous, uncontrolled behaviour, and you have to use skill and discretion to create a reliable verbal 'lead.' If you are too harsh you will again end up with problems, because your dog will learn that life is hard, and will take a similar line in his dealings with everyone he meets – which will result in you not being able to let him off the lead at all.

REMOTE ACTION VERBAL CONTROLS

Expand the basic verbal lead repertoire, which consists of "Stop!" "Come!" and "No!" plus a few rules of particular benefit to you: automatically stopping at every kerb, for instance. You will also need a gesture which will replace the verbal command "Come!" over long distances. This will help your communication system with your dog develop individually without it becoming unnecessarily complicated.

A dog that is used to the lead knows that control over him begins and ends with the lead. For verbal control to be as effective, your dog must learn that this strange form of 'remote control' has to be obeyed in the same way, or he will quickly learn to disregard the verbal 'lead' as soon as he is out of reach. So, when he's standing in the field and not bothering to respond when you shout "Come!" clap your hands sharply or use a clicker or whistle to distract him and get his attention, so that he is ready to listen to further commands.

THE ILLUSION OF PHYSICAL FORCE

You can trick your dog into believing that you have more physical force at your disposal than is actually the case by giving him a demonstration during rough play. When playing wrestling games with him outside, show him that you can, in fact, immobilise him and hold him down. You are scarcely going to be able to leap out of the wheelchair or off your scooter to do the same whilst out and about, but your dog doesn't know that! He will tend instead to rely on his experience of playing with you, which has taught him that you can certainly get physical if you want to. Why you never seem to want to isn't something that he is capable of puzzling out … luckily!

On the other hand if play is too easy-going, and your dog discovers that he can push you around, he will quickly decide that you are subordinate. Play, therefore, is a vital element of your life together, which will establish boundaries, release frustration, and enhance the bond between you. Don't underestimate its value. In addition, in everyday life you can often demonstrate to your dog that you can do things he can't, such as opening a door. That you can hurt him is something your dog will inevitably discover in the course of daily life together, when

you unintentionally roll the wheelchair over his tail or paws, for example.

If, during a confrontation, you do really take hold of him and press him firmly to the floor, this can instil a large amount of respect in him, without you actually having to do anything particularly unpleasant or harmful to your dog.

HEIGHTENED VIGILANCE AND SENSITIVITY

A heightened level of vigilance is necessary for the mobility-impaired person who shares their life with a dog. It is necessary to demonstrate a discerning sensitivity in all aspects of life together, and particularly when any rebukes are necessary. If you spend a lot of time screaming and shouting when out on a walk, you may well end up with a dog who refuses to come back into the house.

Some dogs get panicky at the sight of a polished floor, and you will have a hard time convincing an animal like this to enter the hallway on a wet day. Take note of this kind of thing at an early state and deal with the root cause wherever possible.

These kinds of issues do not suddenly occur spontaneously out of the blue, but instead develop over a period of time, and can be identified at an early stage by behavioural markers that can only be noticed if you are in the habit of keeping a close and regular eye on your dog.

THE IGNORING TACTIC AS A RESPONSE TO PROVOCATION

It will only take a few days for a dog

to work out all the ways in which he can refuse to comply with what his owner wants, and for him to attempt to use this advantage. For this reason, you need to build your relationship on a positive basis, thereby ensuring that situations do not develop where the dog provocatively refuses to do something with the aim of improving his position in the pack hierarchy.

This kind of positive, amicable relationship can be exploited to form the basis of a means of punishment: the ignoring tactic. After my dog has refused to obey me, when he comes to me for attention, I ignore him completely for the next few minutes. In terms of dealing with disobedience, this technique has just as educative an effect as an immediate reaction with a physical sanction. It presupposes that the dog knows it has done wrong, and so always automatically punishes the misdeed.

Although being ignored is unpleasant for a dog – who wants the human to be his friend – it's still a fairly gentle way to correct behaviour when you compare it to other corrective methods, such as electric shock collars, which are completely unacceptable. Observe your dog very closely in order to spot the beginnings of any disobedient behaviour, and act immediately and confidently to correct it.

RELIABILITY AND INDEPENDENCE

Independent conduct, freedom and reliability seem to contradict each other, but that is really not the case, as I have discovered in my many years of dealing with dogs; quite the contrary, in fact. The more freedom I allowed them, the more reliable the dogs became in terms of only operating within that jurisdiction, and not abusing it to gain more independence. A dog who is allowed a long leash, metaphorically and actually, is less likely to resist his actions being restricted for a short time, and is more likely to take a subordinate role when necessary.

WHY DOES MY DOG NEED TO BE INDEPENDENT?

You could make an argument for the idea that a characterless dog, broken by an authoritarian training regime, and which only did anything on command from his owner would be very convenient for a person with restricted mobility, but that isn't the case at all! Instead, the dog really has to be capable of doing things on his own initiative, within a sphere of activity designated by a command from his owner, who is simply too slow and immobile when you compare his ability with a healthy dog's needs for exercise and vigorous activity. It's not possible for him to run around every field, so he must be relied on to go through his whole natural behavioural repertoire – exploring, running, playing, scenting, marking – without any other organized entertainment in the specific field where he has been given permission to do this. The wheelchair/scooter user feels safer on tarmac, or at least paved roads and paths, as it's much easier to get around on these. The dog prefers a soft surface that is gentle on his paws. A dog that can be relied upon to observe the boundaries of his independence can safely separate from his owner, who can direct him to the stream and then let the dog play his own games in and around the water.

Independence in this sense does not mean that the dog is no longer subject to his master's authority. In fact, the wheelchair user has to make his authority even more clearly binding than that of the able-bodied dog owner, who often just uses the lead to 'control' his dog.

This concession of independence implies responsible behaviour on the part of the dog. The basis of this sense of responsibility is provided by an amicable training regime with no battles about rank within the pack. Corrective adjustment of the dog's independence has to be a lifelong, continuous process, just as is the case with training. Otherwise, even an intrinsically submissive dog will slowly work on developing the independence he has been granted into a state of having an entirely separate life of his own, over which it is no longer possible to have any control.

A hefty dose of common sense must be used when granting independence, which must never be confused with being negligent. Repeatedly ask yourself whether you can really justify allowing the dog to act independently and still anticipate all possible reactions. Reliable independence does not just happen. You have to communicate to your dog the specifics of what you expect of him. You cannot allow him out of your sight to enjoy a field until he has proved several times that he doesn't want to lose you. You can only let your dog run loose at the edge of a wood when you can rely on him not to run off after a deer because he feels he is far enough away from you to enable him to do so. Independence necessitates comprehensive and detailed training, and does not mean letting your dog loose to do whatever he wants.

LESS IS MORE

For everyday purposes, at first you need a stop command, which the dog will obey when a few metres away from you ("Stop!"). You need a command to get your dog to come to you ("Come!"). And you also need a general prohibitive command, which you can use to prevent the start of some actions and (possibly) get the dog to stop doing something it has already started ("No!").

Walking to heel happens by itself; your dog doesn't want to lose you along the way. In the canine world, walking next to each other is an expression of affection. So dogs which have not been trained to do this but want to please their owner walk at heel without being instructed to do so. Ensuring that when you are out and about, the dog is always looking to see where you are – and not the other way around! – can be achieved by simply disappearing round the corner or down a hidden turn-off from the path all of a sudden, which an inattentive dog will not notice.

The protective guarding tendency also develops by itself. But this is something that you have to rein in rather than teach your dog.

"Sit! Down! Out! Fetch! Bring!" commands may be fun for games, but they don't provide many benefits in everyday life. If the owner uses them incorrectly, they often end up breaking the animal's spirit in the name of making it obediently submissive.

A SMALL ISSUE WITH FAR–REACHING EFFECTS

As an added bonus, there are a few other areas in which a wheelchair/ scooter user's dog is differently, and perhaps better, trained than one belonging to an able-bodied person.

It is advantageous to train your dog to walk ahead of you, even though these days this is still seen as counterproductive by some experts. If he is ahead of you, you can see him all the time and can intervene more quickly if you need to. Allowing the dog to walk ahead does not interfere in any way with your authority.

It is not advisable to train your dog to walk beside you. Whether he should walk on the left or the right depends on the type of wheelchair, the route you are taking, and the options for getting around badly parked cars, large rubbish bins, and

assorted other obstacles. From a legal point of view, sometimes you are a 'pedestrian' and sometimes you are a 'cyclist.' Because of this confusion, it makes most sense if you train your dog to a general 'by the wheel' command, with a gesture to let him know on which side you want him. This means that when the way ahead is obstructed in some way, he will react intelligently in a manner that resolves the problem, without being an additional distraction. He is able to make his own small decisions in respect of the situation, as he can react more flexibly and more quickly than the wheelchair user, who is slow by comparison.

At an early stage, teach your companion that it is completely okay when people approach you quickly and 'fiddle about from behind you.' It wouldn't be very useful if every person who just wants to help you up the steps, or up a mountain, gets bitten in the backside by your dog …

There will doubtless be other differences to 'normal' dog ownership that arise from your specific circumstances. In my opinion, you can safely depart from the usual path recommended by experts, and tailor your training objectives to your own situation.

UNFAMILIAR OBJECTS

In my experience, if he has never seen one before, the first sight of a wheelchair or mobility scooter tends to unsettle a dog. However, once someone has brought the dog close enough for you to touch him,

WAGGY TAILS & WHEELCHAIRS

he soon loses all fear of this strange and unknown thing, and will come to regard it as an unimportant human toy which does not pose any danger and can safely be ignored.

Because of your lack of height when seated in the chair or on the scooter, you can develop a closer relationship with your dog. Looking straight into the eyes of a big dog can lessen the animal's respect – "You're hardly any bigger than I am!" – but can also lead to a greater degree of intimacy. At this level you can be explored and sniffed all over, and your dog hardly needs to stretch in order to do so. Every dog likes this! This ease of access in everyday life results in permanent proximity to the animal. When I sit on the ground with my dog, I am less reserved in our games; in this position, I am better able to play-fight with him in the way that other canines do. This type of play is something with which he is familiar: he likes having sticks thrown for him, but he prefers the kind of game where there is lots of physical contact.

YOUR DOG HAS TO KNOW HOW TO OCCUPY HIMSELF

An ability to entertain himself is also a form of independence. When you are out exercising your dog, have a break now and then, during which you read a book and don't interact with him. Boredom will cause him to find sticks to carry around, collect stones, and dig. My German Shepherd almost becomes a canine landscape gardener during these breaks; digging up bushes, re-routing streams, building pyramids and messages for alien visitors out of stones he finds lying around – and he seems quite disappointed when we move on …

The benefits of this behaviour are obvious: you don't constantly need to entertain a dog who knows how to entertain himself. As he is always active, he has significantly fewer silly ideas, and is better exercised than other dogs who only move their backsides when their owners force them to.

THE "DO YOUR BUSINESS" COMMAND

Teaching a dog when he can open his bowels, and when and where he can't is much more difficult than teaching perfect walking-to-heel with every imaginable obstacle, as this is about managing the dog's pressing physical needs – which, as a human, it is not always easy to assess correctly. Relating all of the details involved in teaching your dog to open his bowels on command would fill a small book in itself. If you know of a trainer who can do the teaching for you, then I would use him. If you have to do it yourself, you may find the following advice helpful.

As your dog is about to open his bowels or urinate, use a word or expression ("toilet" or "hurry up," perhaps) that he can associate with the function. Do this every time that he toilets so that, eventually, you should be able to ask him to do this on command.

Take time to study your dog to

Ferro finds something interesting to occupy him on the forest floor ...

... and the same goes for in the snow!

determine the times that he usually feels the need to open his bowels; it will usually be fairly regular and the same number of times a day. Use the term or expression that will let him know it's okay for him to proceed. Just doing this will prevent a number of accidents. When you know he really ought to need to go, you can allow him a bit more time. If he ignores all his favourite toilet areas in the afternoon, he must really not need to go, but then will definitely need to in the evening. This enables you to have a fair degree of control over where his leavings are deposited. If a pile does end up where it shouldn't, you can either move it out of the way with a stick, or, with a plastic bag over your hand, collect it up and dispose of it in an appropriate manner.

Whatever you do, don't make such a big issue out of it that he becomes anxious, as then he will not know where he is supposed to do his business.

ROAD TRAFFIC

In our society, a dog needs to be trained quickly to be traffic-safe, particularly in view of the fact that the wheelchair or scooter user mainly uses roads and paved paths. Even in the most rural areas it will be necessary to ensure that your dog has good road and traffic sense.

So, how does off-lead independence work with road traffic? In this chapter, I would like to address a few situations for which the wheelchair/scooter user who has a dog should be prepared, discuss the misdemeanours of other road-users, and highlight how the dog's independent behaviour can be advantageous to all parties concerned.

Once your dog has understood that he is supposed to stay on the pavement whilst you may sometimes travel along the road, he *should* stay on the path. The advantages of this, from his point of view, are that he is

further away from the noisy traffic, and there are all sorts of interesting smells along the edges of the paths. However, he has to learn to walk behind any cars parked at the side of the road, which means temporarily being out of sight of his owner, which he must do without panicking and running out between the cars to look for you on the road. If he's happy to do this, you don't have to constantly battle with kerbs, rubbish bins, illegally parked cars, and other obstructions or obstacles on the pavement, and can use the road, whilst your dog can trot along in traffic-free safety on the pavement.

The prerequisite here is a relatively bomb-proof dog who has been trained to act independently, and an owner who is capable of effectively controlling and halting said dog from several metres (the dog should only begin moving again when his owner moves or gives him a release command).

This is the way I move through noisy city traffic with my German Shepherd, without others even realising that we might belong together. This is significantly safer than making your way tortuously through the chaos with your dog on a lead, which will really slow the traffic and possibly cause other dangers.

It's not necessarily advantageous to train your dog to stop at every kerb, as many situations can be dealt with more smoothly if you don't have to constantly give a release or permission command. Getting around in the wheelchair depends on "letting it roll" in a smooth, continuous motion, so a dog that can be relied on to stop when his owner does, or when he is given the command to stop, makes more sense. Rather than sticking closely to a rigid behaviour, it's best if your dog's primary focus is you.

Now and then, if out with the hand cycle, it can be advantageous to assume the role of pedestrian: when going up slopes or getting through snow on wintery days, for example, you certainly won't be any faster than a pedestrian, so will be better off on the pavement with your dog.

An experienced wheelchair or scooter user will be very familiar with the misdemeanours of other road-users. If you travel along a small country road, keeping to the edge as you are supposed to, other road-users will still see you as a fairly serious safety threat. No one overtakes you, and traffic slows to a crawl. It's conceivable that, in a small town, a wheelchair user with a dog may bring traffic to a complete standstill!

Your dog is much more vulnerable than, say, a person walking at the side of the road, as other traffic seems only to notice the disabled person, and completely overlooks the dog with him.

Study your companion's behaviour very carefully so that you discover as soon as possible in what situations you can trust him. Just as you will most likely have a mental map of nearby surroundings, noting pavements that are too narrow,

stairways, steps and kerbs, you can also pinpoint canine problem zones. Where does your dog, for some reason, have problems with reliability? Where are there other dogs that might attack or trouble him, or that he doesn't like? Where are there cats, sheep, or other chaseable animals which may distract him?

Having this list in your head and constantly being on the look-out and updating your information enables the experienced dog owner to move through critical areas in a safe and controlled way.

Remember, though, that a dog who has once proved himself roadworthy and safe in traffic does not simply stay like this for life. Unreliability will creep back, and you must categorically correct this any time it occurs.

But, if the worst happens, and your dog is on the road between cars, don't shout, as this will draw his concentration away from what is happening on the road and back to you. He will then just hear your commands and come running to you without paying any attention to the traffic. Do not actually move into the road yourself, as then other drivers will only pay attention to you as a disabled person and will not see the dog anymore.

By this stage, sadly, you may no longer have a realistic chance of salvaging anything from the situation; ensure in future you pay better attention and don't let this kind of situation arise.

Dog training for the mobility-impaired

Dog training school?

So far, I have only sketched out the basic guidelines for training your dog, and not explained the practical aspects of how you actually carry out the training. Because so much information is needed to do this, the best advice I can offer is that you read up on this subject from the huge range of literature available, or consider using a professional dog trainer whose techniques and approach you are comfortable with (positive reinforcement and kind training).

My view, though, is that if you study certain basic principles of canine behaviour and the resultant interaction with humans, you can usually process the information so that it relates to your individual situation more easily than if you spend a few evenings at dog training school having a large amount of information thrown at you much too rapidly.

In addition, as a wheelchair user you may not easily be able to implement many of the practical training exercises in class, and probably won't find a standard dog training school that takes into account the special external and spatial requirements of a wheelchair/scooter user, and

also has knowledge of the training objectives that differ from the norm.

You may like to attend the theory sessions dealing with dog training, although remember that, even with this, it may not be possible to put it into practice in the form in which it is taught. My experience is that large parts of the theory are simply of no use to the wheelchair user whatsoever.

So, if you have no background or previous knowledge of dealing with dogs, there's a certain amount of information you must acquire before getting your own. It is often more helpful to talk to someone face-to-face, as they can provide answers to questions very specific to your situation, which a book is unlikely to do. A large number of individuals offer private dog training; they may not be specialised in the needs of wheelchair users per se, but in individual tuition sessions they can advise prospective dog owners about possible problems, and offer training that is closely tailored to the client's personal situation, possibly even visiting his house.

So, here is my recommendation: Yes, to information! And, as for dog training school, not strictly necessary, but sometimes helpful ...

Walks and excursions

Training is a necessary evil to enable the dog to behave in such a way that he will fit into and be part of our society. A kind owner will, when out on a walk, take note of and be guided by the behaviour and ability of his charge. In order to do this, you have to know your dog's limits, but, until you have determined these, here are some basic rough guidelines to help you get on track.

Some vets are of the opinion that an exercise distance of 5 kilometres/3 miles a day is more than sufficient for a German Shepherd, but, in my experience, medium- to large-sized dogs aren't happy until they are covering at least 10 to 15 kilometres/5-10 miles per day. However, that is my view only so my advice is that you do not train your dog to get used to very long walks if you are not able to sustain these, because then he may be dissatisfied with shorter distances. As long as he is receiving a minimum of two walks a day, of at least 30 minutes to an hour's duration, this should be sufficient.

When you are out with a hand cycle, in a racing wheelchair, or on a scooter you will be able to achieve a hiking speed of 9-14kph (5-8mph), which your dog should be able to maintain for some distance.

In a hand cycle you will be faster than in a conventional wheelchair, which means that your dog has to work harder, and is usually keener – after a short break for sniffing around – to start back on the road again. If you use a conventional wheelchair, he may become bored with the lack of speed, but the wheelchair is significantly easier to turn, so renders you more effective in controlling your dog. There are advantages to both modes of transport.

The more relaxed you are when you are out and about with your dog off the lead, the more he will be inclined to act independently – but not necessarily in the way you want him to! Slowing down when going uphill gives more opportunity for canine exploration, and if he becomes bored, he may even rebel if not allowed to entertain himself, or you don't keep him occupied by throwing a stick. The most dangerous situations occur when owners are chatting at the side of the road, whilst their dogs play together. They gradually get further away without their owners noticing – and suddenly are on the other side of the road …

It doesn't mean that you are abandoning your successful dog-training programme if you take your cue from your dog's walking habits and occasionally allow him to spend as much time as he wants sniffing around. Until such time as you have achieved off-lead reliability, you should travel remote, secluded paths, far away from busy roads, dictated by the training that still needs to be done, rather than your dog's walking preferences. If, after a few days of this, you have a choice of routes from which you can assess the reliability of your dog, from time-to-time take your companion's love of nature into account. Moving through a natural meadow, or cross-country in the woods is not very easy or practical, even if you are extremely fit, have a very modern wheelchair or scooter, and the most polished technique. But this is the sort of landscape that your dog loves, and so, for the sake of your four-legged friend, try and include woods, meadows and fields in at least some of your walks, if at all possible.

One way of achieving this is to have your dog go into a field (that doesn't contain any livestock) and then throw a stick or ball into the field for him to retrieve and bring to you on the pavement or road.

Temperature-wise, coldness on walks presents no problem whatsoever for a healthy, active dog, but heat is a different matter, as a dog is only really comfortable at temperatures of up to 12 degrees centigrade/60 degrees fahrenheit. Anything warmer than this results in a reduced willingness to walk, and, if it gets too hot, he will switch off completely.

Devise a walk every day that is tailored to the weather, your inclinations, and the capabilities of your dog by taking into account the following: temperature, speed of the walk, length of the walk, choice of route, and any additional planned activities such as a game ball/stick throwing).

How much wheelchair practice and technical knowledge do you need for night-time excursions? How practiced are you at getting around in your wheelchair or on your scooter? Can you locate a kerb correctly in the dark? Can you transport yourself over a bumpy country track? Can you mend a puncture in the dark?

Every dog owner is sometimes forced to be out and about at unusual times of the day and night, and in the most unpleasant weather, so he must have serviceable technical resources, must be proficient in his driving technique, and have the necessary knowledge and skill to carry out running repairs.

Conscientious checking and care of all equipment is an absolute must: the wheelchair is under more strain at these times, and must therefore be properly maintained to ensure its reliability.

Try and time your walks so that the first one of the day is not taken before 8:00am, when you can more-or-less guarantee daylight all year round, and streets may have already been cleared of any snow or ice. Keep an eye on the weather during the day, so that you can be flexible and bring forward or postpone your walks as necessary.

Likewise, try and make the last walk of the day fairly late in the evening, so that your dog will not have a problem making it through until 8:00am the next morning without needing to go out.

No matter how you arrange it, however, for about six months of the year, the evening walk is going to take place in the dark.

A CAR OF YOUR OWN?

It is not essential for the wheelchair/scooter-using dog owner to have his own car. If a trip to the vet is necessary, this can be incorporated into the day as a walk (if your dog is ever so ill or injured that he can't walk, you would have to get a taxi, but this would constitute exceptional circumstances). The pet shop won't mind delivering to your door, as long as what you order makes this economically viable (order in bulk, if possible).

What is far more important than having your own car is having a good wheelchair/scooter, and a hand cycle that is easy to operate. A dog doesn't want to be driven somewhere and then have just a short walk; he would much prefer to be walking in the great outdoors with you. A car won't make cross-country tracks accessible to you; better to invest your money in the most sophisticated wheelchair you can afford, so that you and your dog can enjoy the delights of this kind of terrain. The hand cycle enables an excursion range of up to 20km/12 miles, which makes a total area of a few hundred square kilometres (60 square miles) in which you and your dog can play without ever getting bored.

The desirability of having your own car can fall anywhere in the range from necessary to useful to completely superfluous, but generally tends towards the latter. A car is useful for food shopping and long-distance journeys; it may even be necessary to have one to get to open country if you live in a town centre, but is really not necessary for anyone who lives in the suburbs or the country.

ALTERNATIVES TO WALKS

From time-to-time, situations may arise that prevent you from taking sufficiently long walks with your four-legged friend. This could be weather-related, a broken wheelchair, or an illness that limits what exercise you can take, which means that a few short walks are all that you can manage for a few days. This won't kill him, but these temporary restrictions will soon result in you having to share your living space with a rebellious, unhappy animal.

However, help is at hand as there

"I'm too tired to run down after it again!"

Falco, a stray who once toured with me, is quite happy with a stone as a 'toy.'

A good time to test out a harness is during your dog's play. Does it fit Ferro properly; does it constrain his movement; is he willing to accept the harness …?

are a few alternative ways in which you can exercise your dog.

● Take some balls, fir cones, or other portable items to the top of a steep slope, and send your dog up and down the hill by playing fetch for a quarter of an hour, after which, he will be happy to curl up in his bed again at home.

● In winter, when you are prevented from going very far because of snow, throwing snowballs and lumps of ice can be to your advantage. Make sure you throw them into a field full of deep snow, so that your dog is literally 'dog-tired' in a very short time.

● If your dog has learnt how to entertain himself, you can relax beside a stream and leave him to do his own thing for an hour, pottering about and digging.

● On the occasions when you are not able or do not want to take him out into the countryside, give him some exercise by way of special toys, such as a remote control car that he can chase.

There are a good many other ways of entertaining your dog – just use your imagination and see what you come up with.

Close emotional ties form the basis of comfortable dealings with your dog, but this kind of partnership can become a problem if you are completely unable to look after

him for any reason, and have to rely on someone else to do so. Actively prepare for this situation by handing over your companion animal occasionally to a friend who would also be able to step in in an emergency.

PRACTICAL ISSUES TO BE AWARE OF

As a start-up guide for beginners, and without making any claims that this list is comprehensive, I'd like to address some issues chosen at random from my experiences, which typify what a dog owner has to deal with, and may help you consider the everyday problems of dog ownership.

● When they encounter joggers or cyclists coming towards them, dogs have the annoying habit of crossing their path to be with their owner right at the last moment, which can result in the cyclist desperately swerving to avoid the dog, or the dog becoming entangled in the jogger's legs. Make sure you call your dog to you in good time.

● A dog that is running ahead or lagging behind will usually walk in the middle of the path. A dog that is walking close to its owner without specific direction, will tend to walk alongside, which means that you are not moving together in a tight group, but taking up the entire path. It is not particularly difficult to counteract this tendency, but you have to remember to take it into consideration and shape your dog's off-lead behaviour accordingly.

• Almost all the dogs I have ever known have been very interested in exploring underpasses and water conduits running under roads. They cool off in the water, and moments later you find that they have run through the tunnel under the road and reappeared on the other side. They will be looking happy because they have found their master again, but, if you have not trained them to obey a "Stay" command, they may well at this point joyously run back to you straight across the road. Watch out for this!

• In critical situations – such as when you are crossing a road – don't allow more than one length of your dog's body between you, and never send him ahead of you to the apparent safety of the other side, Your dog's power of acceleration is faster than yours, and it may be that a car will suddenly appear and prevent you from crossing, whereupon you and your dog are once again separated by a road with traffic on it.

• It may often be the case that you will not be able to cross a road of several lanes in one go, but will have to pause on a central traffic island. It's significantly more difficult to get a dog to listen to a "Stop" command on a traffic island than it is to ask him to wait before crossing a road. You have crossed the first lane at a fast pace and now have to stop him running at exactly the right moment. This is no problem for a well-trained

animal, but most domestic family dogs will not have been trained so methodically, and it is unlikely that this kind of thing could be achieved immediately without an accident. The dog will probably stop, but not until he's already two metres out into the next lane of the road, because he is confused by the intensity of his owner's shouts and by the surprising fact of being asked to stop again. And then it could well be that being surrounded by fast, noisy traffic causes him to fall into a complete panic. In this instance, having your dog on a lead and keeping a tight rein is an absolute must.

• Even on small country roads where there is not much traffic, be very aware of the dangers of your dog maybe running across the road to a dog on the other side, without thinking about hesitating or whether he is being disobedient. Instead of keeping him tethered to you everywhere you go, even on the most remote country paths, ensure that you keep him close beside you where you can easily reach and grasp his halter.

• The edges and corners of roads generally have the most interesting smells, as far as canines are concerned. This can sometimes mean that although you are both crossing the road in a controlled, orderly manner, your dog may suddenly turn halfway across the road because he smelt something good at the last corner, and it has only now occurred to him to go back and have a sniff of it. Result? In just a few seconds, dog and owner are separated by a road. The remedy is as true here as in the previously mentioned examples: be prepared for this to happen and pay better attention in future!

● An exercised and tired dog is generally less aggressive than a rested one, and will tend to more readily shrug off hostile approaches. Interestingly, what your dog has put up with from a more dominant animal – or from you – a few minutes previously, he will happily dole out to a more subservient animal, and will then be particularly sensitive to any provocation.

● Virtually every dog behaves differently in twilight and darkness: some may become more ferocious and some more timid. He may behave differently in many ways, and generally be unreliable and apparently unpredictable. As his owner, you need to be prepared for this and ready to intervene in good time.

● Most animals react to unfamiliar things with fear, and/or refuse to approach them. If you have never used a stairwell before, you may have big problems when having to do so for whatever reason. You might find a kind person to help you up and down the stairs – and then do the same with a trembling dog, who has never experienced steps before.

● If you've never travelled by train you may not be able to persuade your dog into the carriage; likewise with a car or bus.

The foregoing are good examples of what difficulties can occur if your dog is not introduced and habituated to certain everyday things.

Winter: white chaos?

The onset of winter presents those who are mobility-impaired with some tough problems. The self-reliant individual who lives alone can plan his household affairs so that during inclement weather he can stay at home drinking coffee; the wheelchair-using dog owner must leave the house several times a day, even during winter, regardless of how difficult this may be.

Getting out will require a fair amount of strength, a relatively stable state of health, and skilful operation of your wheelchair/scooter (which must be of good quality). Before getting a dog, consider what the previous winter was like where you live. Was there snow on the streets for some time? Did you have very low temperatures for days on end? If you live in a part of the world that receives relatively little snow, you will obviously have far fewer problems.

In areas where the snow lies for more than a few days at a time, it is virtually impossible for the mobility-impaired dog owner who lives alone to get by without special equipment, such as a wheelbase extension for a convertible wheelchair, and a hand

A hand cycle with baggage sufficient for one day: lunch on a frozen lake in Bavaria.

cycle with chains and mountain drive, which it is possible to buy.

On winter days when there has been heavy snowfall, and you can hardly make any progress outside at all, the snow lies so thick in the fields that even the fittest of dogs will be completely exhausted after half an hour of you throwing snowballs for him to chase!

Good, all-weather clothing: waterproof, warming, high-tech, functional wear is a must for being outside – and the mobility-impaired dog owner is no exception!

Once again, it will benefit you to have a dog that has been trained to think independently and entertain himself, as then, hopefully, you have only to struggle a hundred or so metres down the road to the nearest field, where he can run around and play. If where you live does not permit this, you will have to make do with letting him out into the garden, or rely on a kind neighbour or friend to walk him and allow him to do his ablutions, until such time as you are able to get about outside again.

In an area where heavy snowfall or icy roads is usual, organize your dog walks so that he will not need to go for a walk after eight o'clock in

Are you prepared for every kind of weather?

Find yourself something warm to wear in winter that doesn't restrict movement ...

the evening or before nine o'clock in the morning. Between these times, it's probable that the streets will not have been cleared of snow, so there is no way that you will be able to get out and about.

Having to endure the cold for long periods of time can be really challenging to health, as you may be outside for up to three times a day in the most unpleasant conditions, with no opportunity to recuperate. This permanently high level of stress quickly impacts on how much you can do, and then begins to adversely affect your health.

So, in winter, your top priority is to be flexible. A glance out the window will tell you which wheelchair system you need; actual road conditions when you are out will dictate how you get on, and how long you will be outside. Don't plan too much or too far ahead; on many winter days, it's simply a matter of ensuring that you and your dog at least manage to get outdoors and take *some* exercise.

As long as you are properly equipped, winter does not present you with insurmountable difficulties, although it is always a nuisance, which requires resourcefulness to deal with.

And even given the huge headache of coping with additional problems, you and your dog can still enjoy the attractions of a wintry outing, when all is white and still.

The law, your dog, and you

As you will soon come to appreciate, you and your dog are not the only ones living; there are others, too. Dog lovers. Dog haters. A media that tries to discredit dogs and owners with highly biased reporting. Nowadays, dog training is actually the least of our problems!

How you behave towards other people as a new dog owner will affect how you *have* to behave in the years which follow. If you make yourself unpopular early on, you will need to work very hard later to build bridges.

Try and work your way up as quickly as possible to the status of village or town mascot, which will allow you a degree of freedom to do what you like. Demonstrate that your dog – which everyone from bus drivers to shop owners will soon come to know – is obedient and friendly, and that he will stand and wait patiently at the kerb while children ask to stroke him without mummy having hysterics at the very thought. If you make yourself a star in your dog's eyes first, training will be more effective. Then make

yourself and your dog stars in your own neighbourhood, and you will find that you get on so much better with everyone.

A few words about criminality. Are you confident, given your limitations, to be out and about in the dark on your own? When I first looked into the issue of violence towards disabled people, I came to some reassuring conclusions.

Even at the peak of the skinhead movement in the 1990s, virtually all reported attacks on disabled people were invented by the supposed victims in order to draw attention to themselves. If you keep your ear to the ground, you will soon discover that all street fighters, no matter their motivation, consider attacking a defenceless person in a wheelchair to be beneath them.

Only an extreme psychopath would try to sexually assault someone in a wheelchair. This is usually because people in wheelchairs often suffer with ailments and conditions such as incontinence, impotence and bowel function problems, which tend to put off the average sex offender …

And, finally, there is the mistaken belief, which persists to this day, that

"Get off my back, will you? I won't bother you if you don't bother me; all I want is my stick!" A local fighter fowl has Ferro on the run ...

people with disabilities are poor. A number of muggers I talked to gave me the impression that they would let a wheelchair or scooter user pass unmolested, preferring to wait for granny who looks like she has a few pounds in her purse.

The person with a disability is out of bounds, it seems, even for the most hardened criminal, and can therefore walk his dog at night without fear of molestation.

Other dog owners can cause unrest, especially owners of small dogs – and some big ones, too – who don't take into account their charge's personality. "I've got the lead – why do I need to train my dog?" they ask, as they make the dog dance to their tune like a puppet on a string, so creating a conceited, disturbed and aggressive animal who snarls at every dog he meets, and often gets a similar response. This sort of approach and treatment interferes with a dog's natural ability to get on with canines, and other animals, and tars all owners with the same brush ...

The disabled dog owner will find himself bombarded with all manner of 'good' advice. Never react to the sometimes misguided opinions of benevolent know-it-alls who have no real knowledge of the subject. Just sagely nod your head like a nodding dog and keep your thoughts to yourself ...

However, the disabled dog owner can actually take advantage of another form of prejudice. If you are out and about with a German Shepherd or a Retriever, the majority of passers-by will think that you have a professionally trained service dog, and will make concessions that other canines can't benefit from, such as being allowed into shops and on certain types of transport. Only shops that sell food remain out of bounds to you and your four-legged friend because of health and safety issues.

If your landlord is happy to have a tenant with a dog, you're bound to have a neighbour who picks fights as a hobby. If you live in a housing development, it's most likely to be you who's blamed for urine marks, dog mess and barking – even if your dog is completely innocent. You'll maybe encounter the same problem in town and with local authorities. In the countryside, you can be sure that farmers will become apoplectic because they mistakenly believe that their livestock is at risk from dog faeces in their fields. In the woods, you will have trouble with forestry workers and hunters who worry that your dog could frighten the wild animals to death (before the latter has had a chance to kill them himself …), or even actually attack them. Dog-haters are a state-sponsored institution, and every single one is provided with such excellent means of legal redress that they can scarcely resist the temptation to constantly use it against dog and dog owner.

In many countries, the relevant state has encouraged unjustified fears about dogs, thus ensuring that owners are virtually criminalised. Every year the same old discussions rumble on about dog mess, the obligation to keep a dog on a lead, and dog attacks – without ever touching on the important benefits of dogs, and how they help us in many areas of our lives. Dogs rescue people. Dogs deter crime. Dogs help in the home. Dogs can help cure people with mental illness, and detect physical illnesses simply by sniffing. Even the working dog with very little training enables his owner to make new contacts and teaches him about social interaction, which many people apparently seem to have forgotten about these days. He ensures that his owner has a healthy lifestyle by guaranteeing lots of exercise out in the fresh air. The human's friend and assistant, a dog both stabilises and motivates.

And let's not forget his economic significance. Even leaving aside fines, dog owners cough up huge amounts of money every year to pay for insurance, veterinary fees, food, dog training, courses, events, competitions and exhibitions. Only a complete ignoramus – or a government – would dispute this: perhaps they amount to the same thing; I'll leave you to decide, dear reader …

In the interests of harmony, try and see situations from a non-dog owner's point of view, as this may preclude many disagreements. If, however, it should come to a dispute, my advice is not to take a stand until (and if) the complainant produces objective evidence, as many disputes simply peter out for want of hard facts. If you generally behave in a halfway reasonable manner, do not leave a trail of dirt, allow wild barking or make a habit of negligent behaviour in amongst traffic, it's unlikely you will be involved in any serious confrontations.

As the regulation of dog ownership is, in the main, left to the municipal and local authorities, there is always the possibility of special local arrangements. Talk through your situation and its associated problems with the powers-that-be; sometimes it's possible to come to a mutually acceptable solution without a fight, as these days no one wants to be considered prejudiced, or guilty of making life difficult for the disabled dog owner by enforcing rules that are just not practicable. Show willing by doing what you can to comply with existing legal requirements.

Despite the prejudice, aggravation and downright bigotry, owning a dog is fun, provided that you develop the hide of a rhinocerous. To this end, ignore all hostile approaches – whether justified or not – at least until you receive something in writing; a court order, for instance …

Visit Hubble and Hattie on the web: www.hubbleandhattie.com and
www.hubbleandhattie.blogspot.com
Details of all books • New book news • Special offers

Fun and games with your dog!

Okay, then: enough of (in)justice, problems and trouble, and on to pleasant pastimes that you can do with your dog.

ON TOUR

5:30am. It's the start of a warm, summer's day. I roll out of my sleeping bag into the dew-soaked grass: the first rays of sunlight are glinting on the mountain lake. My German Shepherd companion looks at me expectantly, waiting impatiently for me to prepare my breakfast so that he can pinch the sliced sausage off my bread whilst I am looking for the jam in my rucksack. I use the seat of my wheelchair as a worktop for my morning wash routine. The tea is bubbling in the kettle on the camping stove. A harmonious start to a perfect day …

Many dog owners – whether or not disabled – restrict themselves to short walks or days out. But when I was considering a dog of my own, I was particularly interested in the idea

Another beautiful morning on tour.

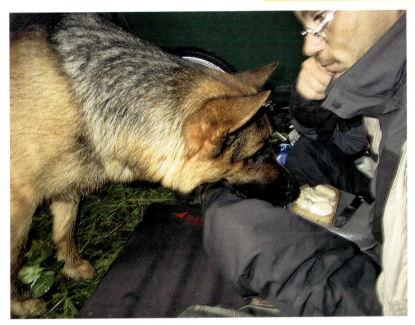

Your canine companion should not steal food. Although Ferro's tummy is rumbling, he does not help himself, but reminds me, by pointing his nose at the cheese sandwich, that I should please not forget about him ...

Hand cycle with touring luggage: all that's necessary for seven days of freedom in the great outdoors.

of having a constant companion for my tours through the countryside: equipped with a bivouac sack and a small amount of carefully chosen, high-quality kit, you can experience absolute freedom for a few days. This type of holiday is just as enjoyable for a dog as it is for a human nature-

Fun and games with your dog!

On tour without a tent. This is a wheelchair compatible camping spot, and the camouflage allows us to merge well with the surroundings (and above, right).

On tour in the pouring rain; hot beverages are crucial for keeping out the cold.

Important points to remember when you are on a trip: lots of breaks; lots of sleep ...

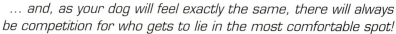

... and, as your dog will feel exactly the same, there will always be competition for who gets to lie in the most comfortable spot!

A perfect spot for an evening swim!

lover, as your dog sleeps, eats and swims in the great outdoors, just as you do.

Breakfast with a cup of tea is later followed by a simple lunch cooked on the camping stove. The early afternoon can be snoozed away lying next to your dog. In late afternoon, you can move on a bit, then spend the evening playing on the shores of a lake; maybe take a swim. A light supper next, and, because it's so lovely there, you decide to stay the night. Holidaying in this carefree way always brings home to me just how much is possible, in spite of poor health, a spinal cord injury, legislation that is hostile to animals, and restrictions wherever you look.

Get close to nature and take the time to look at things outdoors in detail, all the better to appreciate its amazing simplicity.

WHEELCHAIRS, DOGS AND COMPETITIONS

Restricted mobility stands in the way of becoming involved in strictly regimented dog activities such as agility, obedience, and scenting trials, which is why you'd be better off finding other things to do rather than try and force the organisers of these events to take account of your needs in order that you may participate.

The wheelchair/scooter user is completely excluded from most organized canine activities. At a dog show, you may be able to get your dog into the right position, but you will never be able to show him competitively. Any testing of training of protection or tracking dogs assumes a high level of owner mobility, which the wheelchair user is just never going to achieve. You may be offered a special role in

With the best will in the world, there will be some places you just won't be able to go!

proceedings, but then won't earn the officially recognized certificate for skill X that you were aiming for originally. Of course, the wheelchair user can train his dog to scent, but won't win any regimented competition. However, this has nothing to do with actual capabilities as a dog handler.

FUN IN THE WATER

The weightlessness you experience in water makes wild water swimming with your dog a great deal of fun. You can cool off and move around with no pressure on the joints – which is also good for many overbred breeds of dog. If you need some speed, you can persuade your canine companion to give you a tow, perhaps. Most dogs are only too

keen to get into water, if not before you, then certainly once you are in. And, with a spot of training, he will stop trying to drown you and instead swim around happily with you. At a later stage, you can hang on to the sled dog harness that he's wearing, turn on your back and let him pull you along through the water. He will be incredibly proud of what he has done, and your relationship will benefit from the bond that comes from this type of interaction and the trust that it creates.

LET YOUR DOG HELP YOU GET AROUND ...

One dog harnessed by itself as a draught animal is not strong enough to pull a conventional wheelchair.

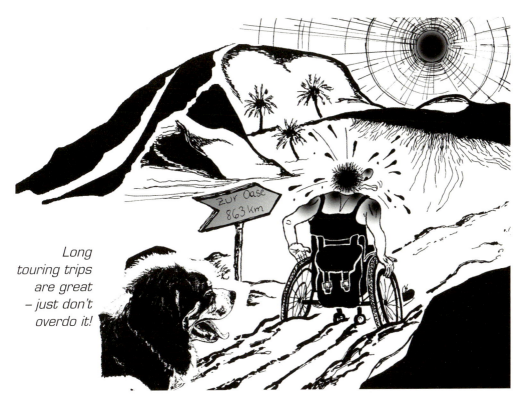

Long touring trips are great – just don't overdo it!

Pulling harnesses for sled dogs; padded and unpadded.

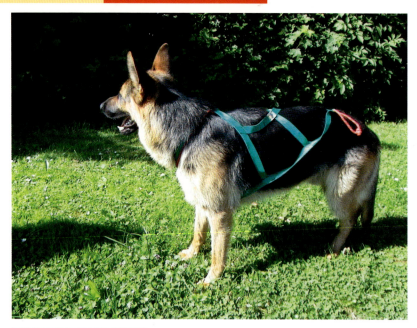

Ferro wearing a sled harness …

A dog can pull you for several kilometres on a luge (sled), or he can pull you in summer sitting on a skateboard with no baggage.

But beware: these kinds of game will definitely make your dog pull on the lead. Even if he previously walked on the lead in an exemplary manner, from the moment he discovers that it's fun to pull, he will pull on the lead all the time thereafter.

... OR TRAIN YOUR OWN ASSISTANCE DOG!

If you prefer intellectual activities with your friend, train your own assistance dog.

Even a beginner soon learns how to get his dog's attention on

… and acting as my 'motor boat'!

Arco

Having your own dog means experiencing nature in spring, summer, autumn ...

Ferro

Layla

a walk, with a gesture in the direction of a stick, and how to give him a verbal command to pick up the stick and bring it to him. With a modicum of patience, this can be extended into a useful service. As you are under no time pressure and don't have to meet any particular criteria, you can spend your dog's entire life developing this training. Mistakes will set you back, but won't hurt anybody if the point of the exercise is more about your dog playing and having fun rather than being useful.

THE FUTURE: WHAT NEXT?

You will quickly come to appreciate that a dog-hater with binoculars doesn't lurk behind every window, trying their best to make your life difficult. In early spring, you will be able to really enjoy being out and about in the great outdoors, feel the sun on your face, the wind rushing around you, and watch your dog running through the field beside the path. A wonderful day, which, if you didn't have a dog, you might have just whiled away at home alone.

Before you take the plunge and get a dog, give serious thought to the problems listed in this book, and try to find practical solutions. Further inform your decision by getting your doctor's considered opinion on the idea of your getting a dog. Your local mobility shop owner will be able to advise you about which wheelchairs will be suitable for the kind of activities you have in mind. Have a look in outdoor clothing and trekking supplies shops for suitable

gear. Talk to dog owners that you know in your neighbourhood about problems with dog ownership specific to your locality, about places to walk your dog, and routes nearby that are suitable for wheelchairs and mobility scooters.

Then confidently put theory into practice by actually getting yourself the dog you have probably wanted for so long …

… and winter, too!

Further reading

You and your Cockapoo: the Essential Guide
David Alderton
Hubble & Hattie (Veloce Publishing Ltd), 2010

You and your Border Terrier: the Essential Guide
David Alderton
Hubble & Hattie (Veloce Publishing Ltd), 2010

Know your dog: the guide to a beautiful relationship
Immanuel Birmelin
Hubble & Hattie (Veloce Publishing Ltd), 2010

Dog Games – stimulating play to entertain your dog and you
Christiane Blenski
Hubble & Hattie (Veloce Publishing Ltd), 2010

The Complete Dog Massage Manual – Gentle Dog Care
Julia Robertson
Hubble & Hattie (Veloce Publishing Ltd), 2010

Dog Relax© – relaxed dogs, relaxed owners
Sabina Pilguj
Hubble & Hattie (Veloce Publishing Ltd), 2010

Dinner with Rover – Delicious, nutritious meals for you and your dog to share
Helena Payton-Ayre
Hubble & Hattie (Veloce Publishing Ltd), 2010

Smellorama! – nose games for dogs
Viviane Theby
Hubble & Hattie (Veloce Publishing Ltd), 2010

Winston ... the dog who changed my life
Hilmar Klute
Hubble & Hattie (Veloce Publishing Ltd), 2009

Friendship instead of dominance – forging a relationship with your dog without shackles
Alexander Epp
Kynos Verlag, 2003

Lassie, Rex & Co: the key to successful dog training
Dr Felicia Rehage
Kynos Verlag, 1999

The other end of the leash: why we do what we do around dogs
Patricia McConnell
Random House, 2003

Atlas of Dog Breeds
Wilcox/Walcowicz:
Thomasson, Grant and Howell, 1990

A WORD FROM THE AUTHOR ...

I am happy to provide personal responses to any questions arising from this book, and relating to the subject of dogs and wheelchairs. I can also deal with questions about bivouacking regarding issues to do with equipment, planning and requirements – or even if you want to join me on a trip!

Alexander Epp
Sportplatzweg 15
(D) 87471 Durach/Weidach
Germany

e-mail: hundskrueppl@freenet.de

More great books from Hubble & Hattie!

Dinner with Rover

Delicious, nutritious recipes for you and your dog to share

Helena Paton-Ayre

Share breakfast, dinner or lunch with your canine friend: this book is packed with scrumptious recipes that you and your dog will love!

Tried and tested by Rover and his friends, and approved by a vet for nutritional value, the recipes in this full-colour book will transform mealtimes!

Paperback • 20.5x20.5cm • 112 pages • 100 colour illustrations
• ISBN: 978-1-845843-13-7 • £9.99

YOU AND YOUR ...

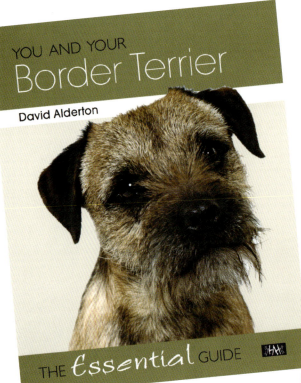

YOU AND YOUR
Border Terrier

David Alderton

THE *Essential* GUIDE

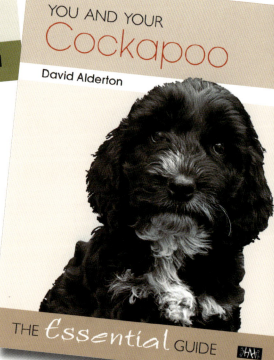

YOU AND YOUR
Cockapoo

David Alderton

THE *Essential* GUIDE

Everything you need to know about choosing, buying and enjoying the dog of your choice, including breed background, settling in your new arrival, establishing a daily routine, and what to expect as your canine companion grows up. 100 illustrations – many specially commissioned – complete the picture.

Paperback • 22x17cm
• 96 pages • 100 colour illustrations
• ISBN: 978-1-845843-20-5 (Cockapoo);
978-1-845843-19-9 (Border Terrier) • £9.99
each

Gentle Dog Care ...

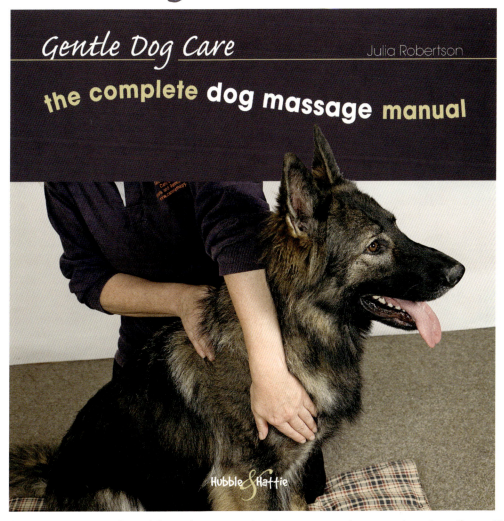

Gentle Dog Care — Julia Robertson

the complete **dog massage** manual

Hubble & Hattie

Demonstrates and explains relevant and safe massage for your dog, together with information about how the dog 'works' in relation to what effects massage has.

Paperback • 20.5x20.5cm • 128 pages • 100 colour illustrations
• ISBN: 978-1-845843-22-9 • £12.99

More great books from Hubble & Hattie!

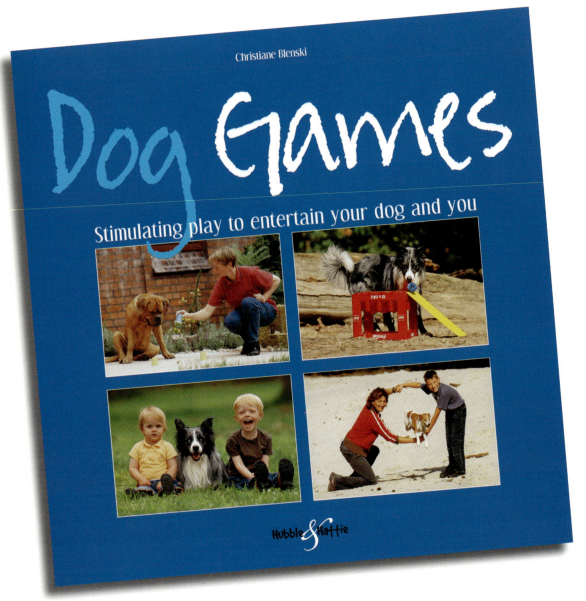

Christiane Blenski

Dog Games

Stimulating play to entertain your dog and you

Hubble & Hattie

New ideas for games that, after just a quick read of the instructions, allow you and your dog to get on with the fun busines of playing. The games in this book will make your dog jump for joy!

Paperback • 25x25cm • 128 pages • 250 colour illustrations • ISBN: 978-1-845843-32-8 • £15.95

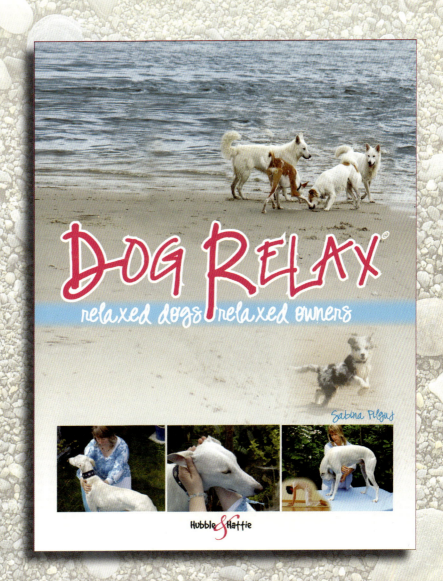

DOG RELAX

relaxed dogs relaxed owners

Sabina Pilguj

Hubble & Hattie

The technique of this book was developed to ensure that both owner and dog are relaxed, via a combination of breathing and movement exercises for the owner, and stretching, movement and special massage for the dog. This lovely book holds the secret to a different approach to living and working with your dog.

Paperback • 22x17cm • 144 pages • 144 colour illustrations • ISBN: 978-1-845843-33-5 • £14.99

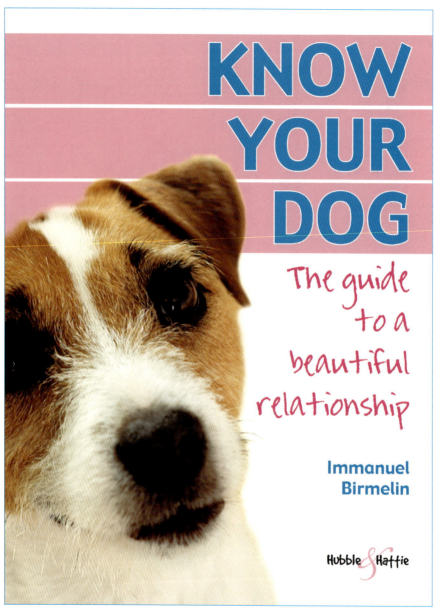

KNOW
YOUR
DOG

The guide
to a
beautiful
relationship

**Immanuel
Birmelin**

Hubble & Hattie

Dogs are thinking, feeling beings; individuals, just as we are, with different personalities, strengths and weaknesses, and distinct emotional lives. Get to know your companion from a different perspective, and understand your dog much better as the relationship between you grows ever deeper.

Hardback • 22x16.5cm • 96 pages • 76 colour illustrations
• ISBN: 978-1-845840-72-3 • £9.99

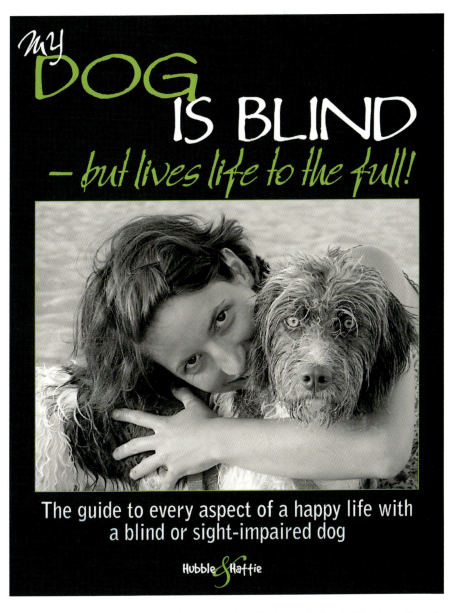

my DOG IS BLIND
– but lives life to the full!

The guide to every aspect of a happy life with a blind or sight-impaired dog

Hubble & Hattie

This invaluable book shows the owner of the newly-blind, partially-sighted or already blind dog that their loyal friend has lost none of her zest for life. With love and careful thought, it is possible to get as much out of life as always, having fun and establishing an even closer bond.

Paperback • 22x17cm • 80 pages • 58 colour & 1 b& illustrations
• ISBN: 978-1-845842-91-8 • £9.99

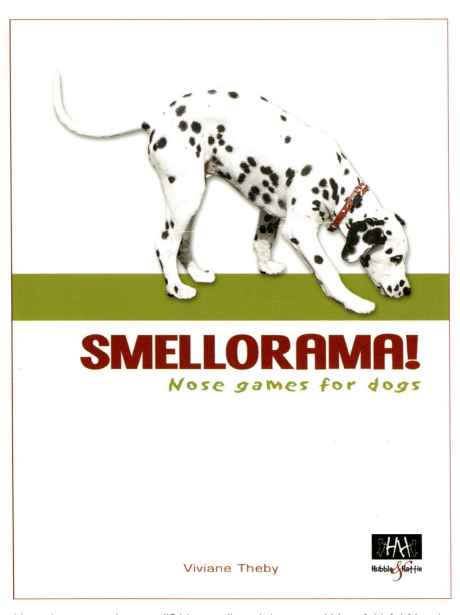

SMELLORAMA!
Nose games for dogs

Viviane Theby

Hubble & Hattie

How does your dog smell? Very well, as it happens! Your faithful friend can be taught to find those lost cars keys, tell you if your food contains minute traces of nuts, or even locate a missing person – and with these nose games, learning how is great fun for you both!

Paperback • 22x17cm • 80 pages • 38 colour & 35 b&w illustrations • ISBN: 978-1-845842-93-2 • £9.99

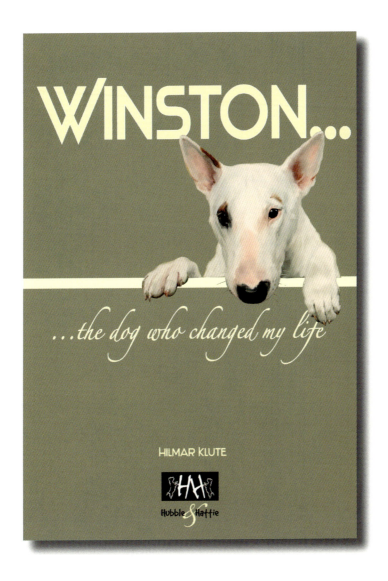

The touching story of how the author rather unexpectedly became a dog owner when his wife returned home with a puppy she had found abandoned in a churchyard. Winston quickly takes over the life and home of his reluctant new owner – introducing him to a completely new world in the process!

Hardback • 12x18cm • 160 pages • ISBN: 978-1-845842-74-1 • £9.99

For more info on Hubble and Hattie books, visit our website at www.hubbleandhattie.com email info@ hubbleandhattie.com • tel 44 (0)1305 260068 • prices subject to change • p&p extra

Index